dancing with disabilities

dancing with disabilities

Opening the

Church to

All God's

Children

Brett Webb-Mitchell

United Church Press
Cleveland, Ohio

United Church Press, Cleveland, Ohio 44115
© 1996 by Brett Webb-Mitchell

Grateful acknowledgment is made to the publishers of the following for permission to use copyrighted material. *Reformed Liturgy and Music* for "The Radical Edge of Baptism," with Stanley Hauerwas. *Reformed Liturgy and Music* for "Teaching Anew the Table Gestures: Children with Disabilities at the Eucharist." *Journal for Preachers* for "Make Way for Electric Blue Wheelchairs!" *Journal of Religion in Disability and Rehabilitation for* "The Abilities Disabilities Make Possible in the Church." *Journal of Religion in Disability and Rehabilitation* for "The Spiritual Abuse of People with Disabilities." *Christian Century* for "Come Unto Me: Children with Disabilities in the Church." *Theology Today* for "Open House: The American Family in the Household of God." *Christian Century* for "Formation and Transformation at Camp Ahus." *Journal of Pastoral Care* for "The Place and Power of Acceptance in Pastoral Care with Persons Who Are Mentally Retarded." *Journal of Religion in Disability and Rehabilitation* for "To Play Is to Care." *Faith at Work* for "The Unexpected Community."

Biblical quotations are from the New Revised Standard Version of the Bible, © 1989 by the Division of Christian Education of the National Council of the Churches of Christ in the U.S.A., and are used by permission

Printed in the United States of America on acid-free paper

01 00   99 98   97 96   5 4 3 2 1

Library of Congress Cataloging-in-Publication Data

Webb-Mitchell, Brett.
    Dancing with disabilities : opening the church to all God's children /
Brett Webb-Mitchell.
       p.   cm.
    Includes bibliographical references (p.   )
    ISBN 0-8298-1152-4 (alk. paper)
       1. Church work with the handicapped.   2. Handicapped—Religious life.   I. Title.
BV4460.W428   1996
261.8'324—dc20   96-38900
                                                                          CIP

To Pam,
who has graced me
with her constant love and love of dancing;
to Adrianne and Parker,
who teach me new dance steps to old tunes;
and to the many other lives
of God's children who
are calling us to the dance of life in Christ

contents

preface

The title of this book, *Dancing with Disabilities*, has a long story behind it. In the many versions of this collection of essays, articles, and sermons, I struggled with finding a title, resorting first to using the various titles of articles already published. The metaphor of dancing was finally affirmed when I saw a newspaper photograph of Mark Edwards, a "runner" I had met in Pennsylvania. In the picture, Mark is leaning on his aluminum walker, his hair sopping wet with perspiration, having just walked the Smith Barney Harrisburg Mile. Mark has cerebral palsy, but in the accompanying article he says: "I have the same hopes and dreams like you do. I want to live my life, just as you do."[1] In the picture, Mark's body looks as taut as any professional dancer's, though his curved posture in the walker would be hard even for a dancer to imitate. For Mark to walk requires an incredible balancing act of will and desire, with his nervous system engaged in a confusing dance of instructing bone, muscle, and tendon to thrust him forward into the intended position. All of this he accomplishes against the backdrop of continually balancing his body with earth's gravity; a never-ending dance. For Mark to travel a mile with the aid of his walker, he must have the stamina of a dancer, for his body demands no less. And he dances on, inviting others in the church, in the world, to join him.

Stories such as Mark's fill most of the pages in this book. "God has graced you with stories," people have told me time and again—people who know me better than I do myself—to the point that I am starting to believe it myself. I have been in the presence of people who have graced me with stories of hope, as well as tales of great anger at injustices perpetrated against them, often by the church. There is no uniformity to these injustice that many people with disabilities experience, but there is some kind of uniformity to their stories. There are stories of feeling excluded because there was no wheelchair ramp leading to the sanctuary; stories of feeling excluded because, even though they had a hearing aid, people still talked too softly and always turned their head at the punchline of a joke; stories of feeling excluded by labels, labels such as "autism" or "Attention Deficit Disorder," labels that—no matter how caringly assigned—kept them out of Sunday school classrooms. Other stories express a wish to be invited to explain to a misinformed congregation or parish how acts intended as charitable can feel smothering, paternalistic, and patronizing.

The diverse writings found in this book give voice to such concerns. They also name the practice of relationships within the church that, whether consciously or not, often exclude the very people we in the church need and desire to welcome. They too are called "children of God."

The opportunity to write these pieces, as well as to present them as papers and collect them into a book, is but a gift of a gracious community of people who also care about me and the issues we raise together. Many people told me to write and speak out on this issue, affirming that, even when I didn't sense it, something important needed to be said, and said *now*. I want to thank my wife, Pam, who, out of love, read and edited these articles, and whose deft ear picked up on what would cause people to think critically or laugh spontaneously. Adrianne and Parker, our children, have been indispensable in welcoming me back with loving embraces and "What did you bring for us?" inquiries after my travels to present many of these papers. They truly make our house a home.

To fellow members of what was once the Muddy Runners Club, Stanley Hauerwas and Steve Long, I owe much, for they listened and responded over countless miles to the ideas in the book, challenging me theologically while supporting my "addiction" to running. Numerous students at Duke Divinity School, too many to count, have heard many of these stories, listened to the logic of my arguments, and still decided to take my courses; they make me not only a good teacher but a better storyteller.

I thank the churches who have listened and responded to some of the sermons in this collection, especially Oakland Presbyterian Church, in Clayton, North Carolina, and Davis Dr. Fellowship, in Cary, North Carolina. It was my joy to meet Cherry Moore of the University of Kentucky, who invited me to a conference that shared the title of the article "Open House." The people of the Covenant Center of Western Carolina Center, in Morganton, North Carolina, gave me an opportunity to see the connection between practices of play and practices of care. L'Arche, in London and Spokane, Washington, taught me much about living Christian community. And the Logan Center of South Bend, Indiana, the University of Notre Dame, and the Synod of the Trinity gave me an opportunity to craft the paper "Politics of Disability."

Kim Sadler of United Church Press was willing to be in conversation with me about this book for a good long time. I thank her and the people of United Church Press for believing in this project and making it a book.

Finally, I am grateful to the families of children with disabilities, people like Sue and Carrot Williams and their children, Rachel and Angie, for teaching me about a new kind of dance. Many people with disabilities patiently taught and teach me about the issue that matters most—that the dance within the church is far more intricate and exciting than I had ever thought possible. But we all know that the real excitement comes only when all who have been created and called by God are welcomed to take their place in the dance of Christian community. In the spirit of Advent, when we await the birth of the Christchild again in our lives, we can wait no longer for the unexpected partners God has already invited to the dance. May this book lead to welcoming—and dancing—with our newfound partners.

introduction

Dancing with Disabilities

You have turned my mourning into dancing; you have taken off
my sackcloth and clothed me with joy, so that my soul may praise
you and not be silent. O God, I will give thanks to you forever.

—Psalm 30:11–12

I watch Rachel dancing, and I find myself laughing with her, for
she dances with a spirit of ease that brings a smile to her face every
time. Often her smile is the dance, for it is an act of the body engaged with music. She often dances with her head and arms, though
I'm sure she will get her feet moving as soon as she gets comfortable in the walker she has just started using. As you get to know
Rachel in the course of reading this book, you will come to understand not only that she lives with what some would consider difficult conditions—mental retardation, cerebral palsy, seizure disorder, and a communication disorder—but also that she has a strong
spirit of determination. This determination has led Rachel's educational evaluators to rewrite her Individualized Education Plan
(IEP) more than once. My hunch is that nowhere in her IEP is it
written that Rachel is a dancer. But it should be—in big, bold letters.

Watching Rachel dance is not my only experience of witnessing
the élan of the dance of children or adults with disabilities. It just
happens to be one of my most striking memories. I am struck not

only by how dancing is a way for many people to express themselves communally, but also by how the apparent effortlessness of Rachel's dancing is evidence that she, as part of a community in which she is loved as a child of God, has been taught the practices that comprise a dance. Rachel dances because the community of Christians in which she has been raised and nurtured practices such dancing of face and movement of body in the context of worshiping God. In that context, worshipers dance, in the words of Irish playwright Brian Friel, "as if language had surrendered to movement—as if ritual, this wordless ceremony, was now the way to speak, to whisper private and sacred things, to be in touch with some otherness."[1] In the dance, we meet Rachel as the child of God she was created to be.

Dancing with Disabilities is about the ever-changing relationship between those people society calls "disabled" and those who are called "non-disabled," in the context of the Christian community. These two groups are locked like dancers in either a passionate embrace or a dance of separateness, trying to move to the rhythm of music that one or the other hears. Sometimes the dance is embarrassingly awkward because of a power struggle over who will lead, who in the church will have the authority to define others and for what purpose. Unfortunately, right now misconceptions overpower willing spirits in the struggle to change society's image of "disability." What remains is unresolved tension over what kind of dance to engage in, and those partners who don't get their way keep threatening to go home.

To complicate things further, the dance partners are tussling with each other over which tune they will dance to—whose language will be used to define the relationship between people who are able-bodied and those with disabilities. Is it right to say "Down's syndrome," or should it be "Down syndrome"?[2] Perhaps we should adopt a new term, "Ups syndrome"? Should people without disabilities be considered "TAB"—*temporarily* able-bodied—a term used by people with disabilities referring to "non-disabled" people? Is it wrong to say "handicapped"? Someone who called me about another book I had written asked, "Why did you use the language 'persons with hearing impairment'? You should have used 'deaf.'

Didn't you have any deaf rights advocates read your manuscript?"

By and large, the church has adopted the language used by health-service professionals and groups who serve as advocates for people with disabilities. By adopting that language, we also adopt strategies and approaches framed by the world but not necessarily by the Gospel of God. Our approach to educating—as well as working with, living with, playing with, and worshiping with—those with disabilities is shaped largely by the rhetoric of the social sciences. Much of what comes out of our denominational publishing houses makes it clear that the so-called disciplines of the social sciences (such as special education and psychology) are determining the church's practices regarding people with disabilities. Thus, not only are pastors and Christian educators embracing the world's *language* to frame the "issues" and adopt the "strategies" of "integrating" people with disabilities into the church, but—by ensuring that the habits we engage in and the politics we are informed by fit the world's definition—we are eagerly adopting the *philosophy* of the world concerning these persons. This is the same world whose health-service practices are characterized by the virtual absence of any discussion of mind, body, and spirit, let alone God.

Sadly, the church offers no language, old or new, to address and thus relate to those the world considers disabled. The church is frustratingly silent about what it may mean to be truly "disabled" or "handicapped" in the presence of God, which may be something radically different from what it means in the secular world. To offer such a new "definition" would require an act of imagination that the church at this time is not disciplined enough to attempt. Daring to ask hard questions and seek a response will fundamentally alter how we may know ourselves. For in the church we assume that we are more than our biological makeup or mental acuity. We are children of God, and individually we are members together in the body of Christ—a far greater and more mysterious reality than we can comprehend but live in anyway. Practicing this truth will mean rewriting how and why we live with one another as we strive to live the good news we share.

If Jesus Christ is the good news of God's love in human form, then how are we to enter into this dance? The first step for all people, disabled and non-disabled alike, is to remind one another of the central truth that, although we may think we are simply dancing with one another, in the context of the body of Christ we are really dancing with Christ. What the poet W. B. Yeats wrote, in "Among School Children"—"O body swayed to music, O brightening glance, How can we know the dancer from the dance?"[3]—is true for us as well. It is impossible to separate the dance from the dancer. Christ is both our dance and the partner we dance with.

Such an understanding of the inextricability of Christ the dance and Christ the dancer means that, when it comes to the dance between people with disabilities and those who are able-bodied, all of us share in this good news that we all "belong to Christ" (2 Cor. 10:7). And none of the labels or categories that purport to describe what one can or cannot do diminish this truth among Christians. In death, Jesus assumed the burden of all our sins, which is good news indeed, since we have all fallen short of God's glory. In the resurrection, we have new life in Christ. In Christ, we continually discover the gift of our salvation, which more genuinely liberates us to discover evermore what it is to be in the greater body of Christ. The love of Christ alone does what we could never do: it makes our "mourning into dancing" (Ps. 30:11). It brings a certain re-enchantment with being human in God, embracing yet again the understanding that we were created in the image of God and called to be children of God as our primary identity.

Of course, this understanding threatens the world's belief that human life is messy and unpredictable. Many in this world have done a great deal to overcome the intimidation of ambiguity by reducing people to "conditions" rather than looking for new ways to live in relationships that recognize our differences. This book asks, What would the practices of the church be if all of us—"disabled" and "able-bodied" alike—were to understand our primary context as a Christian community?

We explore the relationship between the church and people with disabilities in three parts. Part 1 examines the church at worship. It looks at baptism and the eucharist, practices central to our worship of God, practices which cast anew our relationship with one another. Two chapters in this section (originally sermons) attempt to articulate the relationship between people with disabilities and those without.

Part 2 focuses on the church as sanctuary. The particular practices of the church as a living Christian community in its daily life make it a sanctuary for people with disabilities from some of the often hostile practices of the world. How we live life within this sanctuary is a matter of politics within the church. These politics encompass a wide range of issues, from how we will educate *all* Christians to the particular issues of providing pastoral care to people with mental retardation, from stories of confirmation camps in Sweden's Lutheran church to the cry for the church to learn how to accept people with disabilities. All these practices are a response to, as well as a living out of, our worship as God's people.

Part 3 explores the church as servant, engaged in the hopeful, radical practices of serving others in the world. It is through service that we learn to live into—and thus live out—the words of Jesus to feed the hungry, bring drink to the thirsty, welcome the stranger, clothe the naked, comfort the sick, and visit the prisoner.

The relationship between the church and people with disabilities has often been one of much sorrow. I hear countless stories from people with disabilities and their families and friends that reflect much sadness. I pray that this book will give life to the words of Quoheleth, that there is indeed "a time to mourn and a time to dance" (Eccles. 3:4). People with disabilities and their families and friends harbor a great deal of anger about the ways the church has many times been less than welcoming to people who have much to contribute.

There is a point at which mourning starts to become a well-worn rut. I hope this book will not only put a name to the seemingly unquenchable anger that many feel, but begin the process of working out the dance steps that will lead to eventual reconciliation—a reconciliation made possible by the sacrifice of Jesus Christ on our behalf. And what is the song we will dance to? It is the song of Moses, sung in honor of God: "God is my strength, my song, God is my salvation. This is my God, I will praise God" (Exod. 15:2). Let the dance of all God's children begin with this first step.

Part one

The Church at Worship

chapter one

liturgy

Integrating Those with Mental Retardation into the Life of Religious Communities

John Westerhoff III and Brett Webb-Mitchell

Stories from Congregational Worship

In many Protestant churches, young children are welcome in the sanctuary for the first fifteen minutes of worship, up to the point clearly marked in the bulletin as the "Children's Sermon," and then they are dismissed to go elsewhere in the building. Only adults are welcome for the rest of the liturgy. Some Catholic parishes have a room referred to as "the weeping chapel" for infants and their caregivers. The rationale behind such practices goes something like this: Worship would not be entertaining enough to hold the attention of young children, who would then become bored and make noises that disturbed the peace and serenity of others. In some congregations and parishes, people with certain disabling conditions are lumped into the same category as children and excluded from worship on these same grounds. People with mental retardation tell of being relegated to the weeping chapel. Too often, worship is a place and a process where the segregation of people with disabilities such as mental retardation is practiced.

Liturgy, the prescribed use of certain rituals of communal worship in religious communities such as churches and synagogues, has often pulled family members apart rather than brought them together. Not only are children excluded from worship, but so are people with mental retardation, because they are perceived as being unable to understand and enjoy the intellectual breadth of the liturgy, especially the singing of hymns, the reading of Scripture, the preaching, and the recitation of creeds and prayers in unison.

It was seeing people with mental retardation being set aside from inclusion in congregational worship that sparked my interest in the broader issues concerning the church and people with disabilities. When I started working as a music therapist with people with mental retardation in institutions during the 1970s, I was struck by the obvious inconsistency in how the church lived with people with disabilities, particularly those with mental retardation.

Let me illustrate this inconsistency with a story. As a music therapist and a Christian, I worked with some of the choirs of people with mental retardation, all part of an institution's chaplaincy program. The choirs would be invited to visit the churches and perform on certain occasions, usually in the evening, as part of the institution's "community education" plan. On Sunday mornings, however, it was the practice of these same churches and institutions that the facility would have their own worship services for the residents. It was clear that the residents were not welcome at Sunday morning worship, unless they came one-by-one with a staff member from the institution, usually on the staff member's own time and initiative. When I asked why we didn't take all the residents to Sunday worship in the same churches where we had just performed the night before, the response was always the same: "This is the way we've always done it. Why do you ask?"

People with disabilities and their families tell countless stories of being politely asked to leave worship, or in some cases of being *told* not to come to church, with comments such as, "I don't think this is a church where you and your family would feel comfortable."

Yet other congregations and parishes have openly (yet quietly and with little fanfare) accepted people with mental retardation as active participants in the liturgy. I know, for example, of a fifteen-year-old girl named June who is one of the crucifers in a small Episcopal church in Florida. A crucifer carries the cross of Christ in the Episcopal liturgy. June takes her role very seriously, holding the cross high over her head as she walks down the center aisle in her white Nike shoes. She sits quietly with the other worship leaders in the front of the church, calling no attention to herself as she does her part in the morning service.

And then there are Sue and Kevin, members of an Anglican[1] congregation in London, England. Sue and Kevin, who live in a l'Arche community for persons with disabilities, are both active participants in their church. Sue has carved a niche for herself as a peacemaker. Throughout the first half of worship Sunday worship in this Anglican community, all is calm, even rather stiff and formal. Then a change, if not a transformation, occurs during what is commonly referred to as the passing of the peace. With the congregants standing, the priest says, "The peace of the Lord be always with you," and the people respond, "And also with you." At that point, Sue does something simple yet amazing: she turns around in her spot and not only passes but *becomes* the peace of Christ. Amid a rumble of moving feet and chairs, Sue's voice rises above the muffled ones nearby as she says, "How *are* you, darling? It's so good to see you this day, lovie." She hugs every person within her reach, whether she knows them or not, and then, slowly, the rest of the congregation starts to unwind, loosen up, and greet one another with an embrace or a warm handshake. In this church, worship has become celebration.

Sue's friend, Kevin, captures the spirit of the moment during infant baptisms. As the congregation gathers around the baptismal font in the back of the sanctuary, the priest holds the baby to be baptized and recites the words of the institution of baptism for all to hear. Invariably, Kevin gets his face right up close to the unfolding drama of the moment, then he claps and shouts "Hooray" when the priest touches the infant's head with water and says, "I baptize you . . ." Those gathered around the baptismal font smile—as they should for a celebration of welcoming a child into the Christian community.

Reflections on the Presence of Those with Mental Retardation in the Liturgy of Religious Communities

What is happening in the Anglican congregation where Sue and Kevin worshiped is the sign of a Christian community coming together. This community begins to form when one person invites, welcomes, and loves others as they are. This community is the place where people can depend on one another, share their weaknesses as well as their strengths, always being patient with and forgiving one another. For this is the way of Jesus.

This community is both a prerequisite for liturgy and the gift of participating in liturgy. For the Christian community, liturgy is essential, and it is at the very heart of community life. One overriding experience in most liturgies is the experience of celebration, communal joy and thanksgiving. For example, Christians celebrate their coming together and give thanks for the gifts they have been given, especially the gifts of each another. Christians believe that celebration nourishes, restores hope, provides healing, and brings forth the strength to live with the suffering and difficulties of everyday life.

Celebrations sweep away or explain the differences that estrange people; they unite people's hearts. A current of life passes through people as they sing and dance. Celebrations in Christian communities are movements of wonder and awe, when the joy of our bodies and all human senses are linked to the joy of life. Christian communities create liturgies of celebration that bring together music, dance, drama, poetry, art; air, light, water, oil; the bread, wine, fruit, and flowers of the earth; hearing, sight, touch, taste, and smell—celebrations that invite everyone into the community. Such celebration of life, bringing together the various members of a community into a time of drama and suspense, spontaneous joy, and the goodness of life, are evident in the stories of June, Sue, and Kevin.

For June, in the small Episcopal parish in Florida, participating in liturgy doesn't make her stand out as exceptional or extraordinary. This in itself is remarkable. No one focuses on June's Down's syndrome. Instead, the parish has moved to the point of merely accepting her role as an acolyte in the liturgical drama.

And Sue and Kevin, the l'Arche community members, not only thrive on worship, but their fellow parish members depend on them to mark the moments of transformation in otherwise passive rituals. Sue reminds them of the joy of Christ's peace in her all-embracing greetings, and Kevin reminds them of the deeply joyful drama being played out in the ritual of baptism.

These stories underscore the necessity of including people with mental retardation in a Christian community's liturgies. Without their active participation in the liturgical life of a church, there is no chance to witness the reunion of the Christian community with its concept of God and with one another.

Liturgy is the best place to integrate those who are mentally retarded into the life of faith communities. Here people with mental retardation, like anyone else in a congregation or parish, have as much to offer as receive. Still, many adults and clergy people are uncomfortable with the presence of those who are mentally retarded, and some even question how much these persons can benefit from attending worship.

Before addressing these concerns, it might be helpful to reexamine what mental retardation is. The term "mental retardation" denotes substantial limitations in a person's functioning, including sub-average intellectual functioning and related limitations in some adaptive skill areas.[2] The important thing to remember about any definition of mental retardation is that it is a definition of *people*. They are first and foremost human beings, and because they are human beings, they have the capacity to be engaged by rituals like worship. Like other human beings, people with mental retardation are appropriate liturgical participants. They ought to be encouraged to bring their own unique gifts to Christian liturgies. Indeed, the authentic inclusion of those who are mentally retarded will improve a Christian community's worship—as we have seen in the cases of June, Sue, and Kevin—and help also to reform the narrow idea of liturgy that has influenced our celebrations for centuries.

Before exploring further the role of rituals in Christian community, let us define what we mean when we use the idea of "rituals." A ritual is often described by cultural anthropologists and theologians as some kind of stereotypical, repetitive or rhythmic, patterned, symbolic gestures that are understood and practiced within a particular context. A ritual may embody and enact the sacred narrative of the Christian community, forming the people's character. In so doing, those who practice the rituals are being formed by the virtues or moral truths of the Christian community.

Rituals have been divided into three basic categories. Rituals of initiation serve to incorporate people into the Christian community. Rituals of intensification conserve and intensify a Christian community's loyalty and conviction. Rituals of transition or passage highlight the changes in a person's or a community's life.

For the Christian community, rituals help to recall that Christianity is a way of life, rites representing the stories that the community tells itself about itself through consecrated, symbolic social behavior that enables them to live as Christians. Good ritual combines music, dance, rhythmic chant, verbal repetition, poignant smells, familiar tastes, dramatic actions, and impressive sights in the context of ordered time and space.

Christians believe that the sacraments, like baptism and the eucharist, are central to the life of the church; that they are actions of God and signs of God's presence. These rituals make it possible for a congregation to know God, an experience to which those who are mentally retarded may also be open—because the meaning of the sacraments does not depend on intellectual reason. For too long many Christians believed that one has to understand the sacraments before one can experience them. Many in the church now realize that the converse is true: that one needs to be engaged by celebration of the sacraments before one can understand them. Of course, no one fully understands the sacaments, which makes them a divine mystery that speaks to the heart in spite of human intellect.

During the Enlightenment there was a rediscovery of reason and verbal communication, which explains why most Protestant worship still relies on the spoken word, the intellect, passivity, and individualism. For many, the only liturgy they know is singing a few hymns, saying a few prayers, and listening to a long sermon that is frequently tedious and uninteresting, the major purpose of which is to clarify right doctrine and explain the reasons for right behavior. In their desire for reform they threw out the baby with the bath water. Today they are acknowledging that the best way to be faithful to their past is not to continue it, but to be as faithful to the needs of their day as their forebears attempted to be in theirs. In doing so they have looked to the early church for clues regarding worship and good liturgy.

Defining "Good" Liturgy

Liturgy is concerned with the patterns of behavior being shared among a group of people. It is not the rhetoric of only a sermon, or just the experience of the worshipers, but the communal celebration of the event that is important. Christians believe that the emphasis is less on the mind and more in the spirit or the heart. Therefore, liturgy is something that a community of people gather together to participate in, not just with their mind, but with all that they are: body, mind, and spirit. Hence the importance of their gestures and movements of sequence of the seasons, of the use of all the senses and all the creative arts.

The key to liturgy is in its performance. Liturgy is a matter of significant actions that suggest meaning. Because it goes beyond intellect like speech and reading, liturgy impresses on the participants the importance of the inarticulate and that which is considered intuitive. It provides a context for words and actions to be repeated over and over again, thus enabling the participants to participate beneath the surface of events, to mind, body, and spirit.

The anthropologist Victor Turner commented that human beings depend on rituals to provide structure and order to an otherwise chaotic environment. Rituals are necessary to life in Christian community; they provide a sense of security, cohesion, meaning, purpose and aim for life.[3]

Having a sense of the aim of life is often overemphasized on the cognitive mode of consciousness, or of knowing, that has contributed to the demise of knowing as an act of mind, body, and spirit, and has contributed to a sickness in the life of many Christian communities. It is the significance of the word of symbol, myth, and ritual that must be recaptured in our day and in our churches. Christian symbols comprise action symbols (sacraments), narrative symbols (myths or sacred stories), and language symbols (words). Still it is the experience narrated by the Christian story itself that is essential, and without the experience and narrative from which the symbol emerges and to which the symbol points, words remain empty conceptual verbalizations requiring definition and having no power over present circumstances.

Edward Robinson, in his book *The Original Vision*, reports on his findings concerning the religious experience of childhood.[4] Few books offer greater insights for understanding religious life and spiritual awareness. To summarize their findings, a significant number of persons report having significant religious experiences as young children through nature, the arts, and participation in religious rites, but testify that they were unable to name, describe, explain, or understand these experiences until much later. Because children could not talk about their experiences, it was assumed they did not have them.

In conclusion, Christian thought is grounded in experiences with the Christian story. Christians' conceptualizations of God are grounded in their knowledge of God. Their encounter with God is expressed, communicated in, and nurtured through dance, music, drama, poetry, painting, sculpture, and film; and through the stimulation of the imagination by our visual, oral, and kinesthetic senses. Such moments and the arts are related. So are such Christian experiences and the liturgy. The distance that many have put between themselves and the arts in Christian communities like the church has impoverished their religious experience and diminished the effectiveness of their liturgies.

Implications of Liturgy for People with Mental Retardation

People with mental retardation yearn to participate in the liturgies of Christian communities like the church. This was true of June, who as an observant and conscientious crucifer found her place in the liturgy of her church. Likewise, Sue and Kevin revealed to others the special moments of worship.

There are still those who conceive of the Christian faith solely as an appeal solely to the mind, the "objective," "rational" dimension of human life. Therefore, they assert that saving faith is best understood in terms of intellectual assertions of the truth of par-

ticular propositional statements, and they have difficulty comprehending liturgy as symbolic action, cosmic dance, or operatic drama.
Liturgy that shapes our perceptions and character through the use
of art, poetry, drama, dance and music; through sight, touch, taste,
smell, and sound; through the repetition of symbolic words and
actions is difficult for them to understand or accept. Many adults
want their liturgy to serve a didactic purpose, and since lengthy
intellectual, doctrinal sermons are their major concern, they con-
clude (rightly) that worship is not an appropriate place for people
with mental retardation. However, it is this understanding of worship that needs to be seriously questioned, not the appropriateness
of people with mental retardation participating in worship.

The Western world has developed into a low-context, ocular
culture that values rational statements and the printed word, and
in turn depreciates the context, style, tone, and nonverbal expression of the affect and passion. It also depreciates the oral culture's
involvement of all the senses, in symbol, myth, and ritual, and values solely the eye reading, writing, reason and in worship that is
detached, heady, and didactic behaviors, often leaving people with
mental retardation closed out of congregational worship.

In the church, it is believed that through worship unity of the
church, the household of God, is realized in Christ. As a matter of
justice, no one should be barred from that unity. That is why liturgy is at the center of our life in the church. The church believes
that worship is the particular vocation or calling; no Christian is to
be barred from liturgy, no baptized person excommunicated from
the church; hence, people with mental retardation belong in worship. Those who are mentally retarded, if they are to be shaped as
Christians, need to participate fully in the church's rituals.

If people with mental retardation find the church's rituals mean-
ingless, perhaps the church should change the liturgy rather than
make those with disabilities sit silently through it, or worse yet,
have them leave. Those who are mentally retarded, like anyone
else, are open to the mysteries of life; they learn through play, imagination, and creativity. Many approach the world intuitively; they
too can understand liturgy as holy play, as godly play.[5]

Jean Vanier, the founder of the l'Arche communities for both those who are mentally retarded and assistants, wrote this about celebrations: "I have always loved what the king said to his servants in St. Matthew's Gospel: Go to the thoroughfares and invite to the wedding feast as many as you find" (Matt. 22:9).[6] We are not made to be sad and to work all the time. We are invited to the wedding feast! Our communities should be signs of joy and celebration. If they are, people will commit themselves with us. Communities that are sad are sterile; they are places of death. Of course our joy on earth is far from complete. But our celebrations are small signs of the eternal celebration of the wedding feast to which we are *all* invited.

chapter two

the radical edge
of baptism

Stanley Hauerwas and Brett Webb-Mitchell

What's so radical about baptism? For many members of mainline Protestant churches, there is little that is special or necessarily radical about baptism. Many new parents, particularly those who left their respective churches shortly after completing confirmation classes in junior high school, have been returning to church with their own infants and children in tow. One reason for this return is that they remember (or are reminded by their parents) that baptism was "done to them"—as if it were a custom of the family rather than an act of a congregation. Baptism is thus reduced to a social fashion, the thing to do, what chaplain J. A. Davidson describes as a "social event, becoming a pagan birth festival or a bit of pious baby worship."[1] Still others confuse baptism with an "act of dedication," the seeking of a "divine blessing" not only for the child but also for the parents, who are seen as the primary agents for nurturing the child in the Christian faith. The "real baptism" will take place later in life, when the child decides that he or she wants to be baptized.[2]

Amid this confusion about the meaning of baptism in the life of the church, the radical nature of the common things Christians do is lost because we have become accustomed to them. It is right, of course, that these things are common, as it is the purpose of the gospel to make our lives communal. Indeed, it is fascinating to consider the relationship between the common and the communal: it is through what we have in common that we become a community. Surely baptism is the sacramental act that signifies most clearly what Christians share in common—that is, the death and resurrection of Christ:

> Do you not know that all of us who have been baptized into Christ Jesus were baptized into his death? Therefore we have been buried with him by baptism into death, so that, just as Christ was raised from the dead by the glory of [God], so we too might walk in newness of life. (Rom. 6:3–4)

Through baptism, God creates the church and gives the church its originating action. So baptism is at once the church's possession and yet not ours to possess. Baptism is the work of the Spirit, an unquenchable fiery Spirit who births a people who would otherwise not be God's people. Saint Peter said:

> Repent, and be baptized every one of you in the name of Jesus Christ so that your sins may be forgiven; and you will receive the gift of the Holy Spirit. For the promise is for you, for your children, and for all who are far away, everyone whom God calls. (Acts 2:38–39)

Through baptism we discover again that we are not our own. For Christians, it is the most determinative act of God's creation.

Controversies concerning infant versus adult baptism pale next to the discussion of the significance of baptism itself as it is understood in the Reformed tradition. This sacred action of God is a sign for us Christians, children and adults alike, aiding us in the recognition that God is doing something here and now, for all to see and hear, awakening us to the dawning realization that we are incorporated into Christ.[3] The Reformed theologian John Calvin quotes St. Augustine, who wrote that because we are flesh, we have a dull capacity and need to be led by the hand "as tutors lead children." This sacrament is a "visible word" for the "reason that it represents God's promises as painted in a picture and sets them before our sight, portrayed graphically and in the manner of images."[4] Baptism intensifies what God was already effecting prior to the sacrament itself.⁵ Both divine and human agency have been in collaboration as this new person is progressively informed with the power, wisdom, and love of the God his or her parents worship. John Calvin made it clear that children will grow into an understanding of their baptism:

> If they happen to grow to an age at which they can be taught the truth of baptism, they shall be fired with greater zeal for renewal, from learning that they were given the token of it in their first infancy in order that they might meditate upon it throughout life.⁶

Baptism is the seal of what the Word of God proclaims—that we are forgiven and made part of a reality, "grafted into Christ forever," marked as Christ's own,⁷ that we could not imagine unless it was God's doing. The Reverend Susan Allred likes to say, "This is God's church, because I could have never thought of anything so imaginative as the creation of something called 'church.'" Baptism makes this reality possible and thus is a comfort for all those who have been baptized into Christ. Baptism "gives the church its identity and commissions the church for ministry to the world."⁸

No issue illumines the radical character of baptism more clearly than baptizing those who are "mentally retarded."⁹ In their baptism, we recognize anew our own status before God. In the baptism of those with mental retardation, the rationalist presumptions so prevalent in modernity concerning the Christian faith are undercut. What does it mean for us to understand what happens in baptism when God has made it possible for those who cannot understand to become part of God's people? In the prismatic act of baptism of those who are considered mentally retarded, we can see our very own lives enacted in a bold and audacious manner. Consider the lessons learned by baptizing those who are profoundly mentally retarded.

First, we recognize that this is not an innocent initiation rite of children into a naturalistic community. Rather, in this action of God, we become part of Christ's body, God's people, being made part of a story not of our own creation. That is why, in baptism, we acquire our true names as children of God (Rom. 8:6). We are reminded that, in baptism, we cannot name ourselves; rather, we become what God and the church would have us be. That is why we must continually be reminded of our baptism, for it can happen only once, though there are many times in worship when we acknowledge the grace of God continually at work in our lives.[10] That is why it is such a decisive event, like birth, even though we are tempted to deny its existence. We must be reminded of our baptism and, in being reminded, we will discover and rediscover that we are not our own makers. Instead, we are created by God, who calls us God's children.

Second, this act of naming us "God's children" is not performed by the individual being baptized. Simply put: we cannot baptize ourselves. Baptism stands out as an act of the Christian community we are called to; God works through the lives of the members participating in the sacrament of baptism. Theologian John Baillie writes that decisions are being made for the child—by his parents, by the church—and these decisions cannot be postponed, because life goes on and the child grows up one way or the other. In baptism, the church chooses the Christian life for the child.[11]

Baptism involves our relationship with God through the very act of touching one another—in laying-on of hands, speaking face-to-face, and pouring ordinary water—to underline the extraordinary God who is present with us in this sacramental act. In baptizing persons who are mentally retarded, our minds become their minds, and their bodies become our bodies. Through the baptism of those who are mentally retarded, we recognize that we do not know who we are until God tells us by making us members of the communion of saints. Indeed, in baptism we are made saints. And part of that telling is the discovery that I cannot be who I am without the lives of those who are mentally retarded.

Third, the act of baptism exposes with brilliant clarity the difference between church and world. Baptism brings us into a new environment, the environment of the church of Jesus Christ, which will surround us, form us, and nurture us into a deeper dependence on the diverse members of the body of Christ. This, of course, is an extremely offensive set of claims, particularly these days when we are taught to believe that we are or should be independent and self-creative people capable of forging our own stories. Modernity wants us to believe what theologian John Baillie called a "false individualism," the belief that the child is an independent soul, able to grow without the constant love, guidance, and nurture of the church.[12] Baptism is an affront, a challenge to our presumption that we are our own creators. A church that is shaped by baptism cannot help but finally be a church that should threaten our world and its presumptions.

Instead, baptism as an act of Christ's community rather than that of an individual person should be a comfort, especially for parents of children with profound mental retardation. Those who participate during the presentation of an infant or child promise that, as members of the church of Jesus Christ, they will "guide and nurture the child by word and deed, with love and prayer, encouraging the child to know and follow Christ and to be a faithful member of his church."[13] Uttering these words, those assembled are now accountable to one another—and to God—for raising the infant or child with the aim of becoming a faithful member of Christ's church. No longer is this child perceived as an individual, independent person; he or she is now viewed as a child of the New Covenant, to be raised in the Christian faith not only by his or her parents, but by the congregation as a whole.

The church will no doubt need to be reminded that it is truly its brother's and sister's keeper, refuting the example of Cain (in Genesis 4:9), who followed the human temptation to avoid responsibility for others. For the parents of children with mental retardation, the good news is that they are not the sole nor the primary agents responsible for raising this child in the church. No longer is this child the child of its parents. The child with a disability is a child of God, a child owned by God, and God cares for that child through the act of the community of Christ as a whole. This child is an important and interesting storyteller, participating in the ongoing narrative of the Christian faith.

What may not be a comfort to some is the knowledge that baptism initiates us into Christ's death and resurrection. The knowledge that this is our true death enables us to live courageously without fearing the death that the world offers. In the sacrament of baptism, we turn "from the ways of sin and renounce evil and its power in the world," and instead turn to Christ, accepting Christ as Savior, and thus hold onto the promise of life everlasting as uttered in the Apostles' Creed.[14] In this renunciation and profession, Christians can envision the death of children, because we know through baptism that they have been made all they will ever be. Thus, Christians could take their children to martyrdom rather than leave them to be raised pagan because they knew it was better to die Christian than to live the life of the pagan.

In our culture, Christian baptism seems offensive, for nothing embodies our culture's sentimentality more determinatively than the presumption that our children do not have to suffer for our convictions. As Christians we believe that, through baptism, our children have become, as we have, part of Christ's death and resurrection and are thus ready to combat the world. Of course, we desire life for our children, but we desire even more that they, like us, be faithful to what has happened, is happening, and will happen to our lives in Christ through baptism.

So let us bring our children and those who are disabled and ourselves to baptism. It is a common act, commonly done, that constitutes God's people for a world that worships not our God. Without this sacramental act, we literally could not be. But through baptism we become the kind of beings that make possible the good news that, through and in Christ, we are made members of God's people so that the world might know that death has been defeated. And this is radical indeed.

chapter three

teaching anew the
table gesture

Children with Disabilities
Sharing in the Eucharist

What is a table gesture? And what does it have to do with children
with disabilities sharing in the eucharistic celebration of the church?
In her book *Worship*, Evelyn Underhill offers an interesting description of the way early Calvinists celebrated the eucharist. John
Calvin, she observes, understood this meal to be the "holy meat
and drink of eternal life."[1] He believed that, although the elements
themselves did not embody Christ, God's Spirit was nevertheless
engaged in and moving about (if not "brooding over") the meal—
thus making it a truly supernatural experience for one and all. Celebrating this sacrament in the early Calvinist churches, people came
forward to the front of the sanctuary and

> sat or stood at a table, and shared the one bread which was broken
> from hand to hand: thus restoring to Christian custom the ancient
> and precious symbolism of the One Loaf. This is the so-called Table
> Gesture: now generally and unfortunately abandoned in favor of a
> distribution of the elements to communicants seated in their pews.[2]

The Presbyterian Church's *Book of Common Worship* declares that
the actions of breaking the One Loaf of bread and pouring the
juice of the vine "should be clearly visible to all present."[3] The One
Loaf broken and given to the people of God who gather around
the table, as the words of institution are being said, is a reminder,

we are told, that Christ's body was broken for all of us, regardless of our abilities or limitations. And Christ's blood was shed for us and our salvation, regardless of our abilities or limitations.[4] The gestures of this meal remind us in vivid detail that a sacrifice was and is made in our name and for our sake, because of our sinfulness and unfaithfulness, and as a divine gesture of God's faithfulness and love made incarnate for all generations.

The breathtaking sweep of this universal, eternal meal to which we are invited is illustrated by a story of events that took place at Montreat Conference Center in the summer of 1995. This is the story of Rachel. Some days Rachel can be a charmer. She has her father's red hair, her mother's round face, and eyes that lift up, as if looking into the sky, sometimes catching you unawares that she is looking at you. She has a delightfully appealing sense of humor that invites friends and family to make her giggle or laugh at the slightest or silliest provocation, (whether there's food in her mouth or not). Rachel sits in what appears to be a comfortable position in her wheelchair, harnessed well enough that she won't fall out and hurt herself or anyone else. She is learning to use a computerized board for communicating, as well as a custom-fit walker that allows her to walk without holding on to anyone else.

Rachel, who recently turned five years old, is a child whose gifts and talents have not yet found expression in a congregation because of various limitations that encumber her participation. Rachel is labeled mentally retarded; she has a physical disability, a speech impairment, and some seizure activity; she loves to laugh and shriek, which seems to be her way to communicate much of what she is thinking and feeling. To say the least, she makes the community we Christians are called to be part of interesting.

I spent a week with Rachel and her family at the Family Conference at Montreat Conference Center. During that week, the participating children and the adults shared creative times of worship together each evening, experiencing everything from the ritual of foot and hand washing to a renewal of baptism. On the final evening, hungry and tired children and adults assembled for the eucharist with store-bought grape juice and loaves of bread. It was here, in this time and place, with these members of Christ's body, that Rachel pulled out all the stops and surprised everyone around her, including her parents, who thought they knew her well.

Rachel's father, Carrot, had taken Rachel out of her walker and was physically leading her to the front of the line in which others were partaking of bread and juice. I was holding the half loaf of baked bread when Rachel, with purpose in her step, came lurching me, lifting her head every now and then to see where she was. Carrot held her by the right arm, while David, another parent in the group, held her left arm, and this steadying of her movement was a loving act of walking *with* and not *for* Rachel.

Partaking in this ritual was truly an act of community, with all four of us working together. Carrot tried to guide Rachel's hand over to the bread I was holding up to her. Suddenly, with no verbal cue whatsoever, Rachel's hand shot out to the bread, and her fingers grasped a bit from the loaf I held in front of her. Then, with little help from David and Carrot, she dipped the bread into the cup of juice held by the elder serving with me, and took the bread into her mouth *all by herself*. This was the first time Rachel had ever participated in such a voluntary way in this sacramental ritual, and the significance of the moment was not lost on anyone gathered there. Carrot said later that all he had wanted to do afterward was hold on to Rachel, so moved was he by his daughter's surprising gesture.

In Luke 24:13–35, the disciples who are traveling to Emmaus recognize Christ only in the act of breaking bread. Christ's miraculous Spirit was made known to us that evening in the breaking of the bread in the hands of a remarkable five-year-old. At birth, Rachel's less-than-hopeful clinical prognosis stated that she would never be able to make the kind of progress she has displayed in her motor and cognitive abilities. We all thought we knew what Rachel *couldn't* do, but at *this* meal, our eyes were opened to what Rachel *could* do with the support of her community of Christian faith. Rachel's unexpected gesture revealed to us all God's love made manifest in the eucharistic celebration, re-membering us all, young and old alike, into the body of Christ.

At this table, in these gestures around the bread and the cup, the eucharist became a new way of seeing and hearing the world and every one of us in it, including Rachel and other people with distinctive differences. And what did we see that changed how we look at one another? We saw God moving in the stories of people's lives, reminding us that Rachel—like her parents, and her parents' parents—is created in the image of God. Made in the image of a God who created us to be in relationship, we are therefore not created as private selves utterly detached from a community.[5] We are created with a purpose in God's mind, chosen for a place in the body of Christ. In the eucharistic meal, we get a foretaste of what it means to live together in lives that are located in and given meaning by the very gestures practiced at Christ's table.

Theologian Stanley Hauerwas argues that the church's liturgy is social action: "Through liturgy we are shaped to live rightly the story of God, to become part of that story, and are thus able to recognize and respond to the saints in our midst."[6] The "Invitation to [Christ's] Table," in the *Book of Common Worship* tells us: "This is [Christ's] table. Our Savior invites those who trust [Christ] to share the feast which [Christ] has prepared."[7] These words encourage us and instruct us how to live with one another, especially in terms of sharing worship with those who, like Rachel, have been shunned from the table by narrow understanding. The opening words of the "Invitation" show us how our perceptions of—and relationships with—children with disabilities are shaped. These words also show us how the perceptions of these children and their relationships with us are shaped, even transformed, as we perceive one another through the practice of the eucharist.

"This is [Christ's] table." This simple declaration of whose table we gather around is key to our understanding of everything else that occurs at, and because of, this table. Too often we act as if this were *our* table, open not to all who have been baptized but only to those who meet some test of earthly ability. We erroneously assume that the sacramental mystery of God can be appreciated only by those people whom society considers "normal." Frederick Buechner questions this assumption: "When it comes to the forgiving and transforming love of God, one wonders if the six-week-old screecher knows all that much less than the Archbishop of Canterbury."[8]

For children with disabilities, physical, emotional, mental, or sensory differences may sometimes overshadow remarkable abilities which go unnoticed in an uncomprehending world. No limitations, real or perceived, should interfere with our purpose for being in church—to glorify and enjoy God forever.[9] We need children with pronounced differences at the table with us, because they are reminders that the church's primary purpose is to bear witness to the sovereignty of Jesus Christ. Children with differences, by participating in the gestures around Christ's table, can provoke our numbed imaginations in wonderful ways.

All children need the good news of Jesus Christ and the promises of the new covenant. All children also need to be baptized, with the sign and seal of God's grace made public for the entire community to see, hear, feel, and be moved by. When we focus on the disability of an individual child, we lose sight of the human being whose significance is located in the Christian community.

"Our Savior invites those who trust [Christ]." The divine initiative is heralded in the beginning of this sentence. "Our Savior" is the one who extends the invitation, an invitation that can only be heard by those who trust in Christ. This initiative is probable because Christ is more fully expressed in the Christian sacraments.[10] Citing the work of John Calvin, theologian Nicholas Wolterstorff writes that, as we enter into the liturgy in the celebration of the sacraments, we enter the sphere "not just of divine presence but of divine action. God, in Calvin's way of thinking, is less a presence to be apprehended in the liturgy than an agent to be engaged."[11] In the sacrament, we know more of Christ through the drama of God offering us bread and wine, Christ's body and blood, and our eating and drinking these very things.[12]

One metaphor that might help us better understand our posture before God comes from theologian Rodney Clapp, who writes that children "unashamedly confess their need for others." They are, he writes, "suckling babes as moral models."[13] Like any children, children with disabilities need others. Many children with disabling conditions need more than other children in the way of health and social services; this dependence we take for granted.

At the table, seeing children with disabling conditions, we come face-to-face with our own dependence, which is not exactly an easy thing to do in a society that celebrates the sovereignty of the autonomous individual. Despite the elaborate precautions we take to guard our personal lives, we will eventually face our own dependence.

"... *to share the feast which [Christ] has prepared.*" Sharing this feast, which was prepared not by us but for us, calls forth a kind of community that both comprehends the significance of the meal and desires to earnestly sustain its practice. Sharing is not in our nature—it defies our inborn selfishness—but by sharing this meal established by Christ, we focus on the true nature of our calling to be part of Christ's body. We celebrate this meal because it is a means of faithful service to Christ and to the world.

Children with disabilities (and all of us) need to learn not only *how* to share, but also *why* to share, absorbing from experiences around them the very ways we share. We who are in community with these children are given the opportunity not only to share, but also to practice the pattern of sharing, to rehearse again the story that guides the gestures.

Children like Rachel, children with differences, allow us a taste of the heavenly banquet that may be unlike any food we have experienced before. By God's own choice and design, Rachel is part of God's realm, and she has a place in the body of Christ. This is going to be a noisy gathering—what with wheelchairs, crutches, and aluminum walkers being scooted forward. There may even be a scream heard as a child with fetal alcohol syndrome, frightened by blood, hears for the first time that this is Christ's blood. This is the communion of saints gathering together, one more time, around bread and wine. And God, who knows how to make noise and silence, is engaged with us all.

If the "taste" and "sight" of the Table Gesture, this banquet feast, is uncomfortable with such brilliant difference, it is most likely because our palates are too immature, our vision too narrow. Thanks be to God for children like Rachel, who give cause for more discerning palates and a widening of our lenses. For without such children, we may fail not merely to see children like Rachel and their invaluable contribution to shaping the very virtues of this community's character, which are the marks of life in Christ. More seriously, we may fail to see Christ, who told us that "just as you did it to one of the least of these who are members of my family, you did it to me" (Matt. 25:40).

chapter four

practice your hearing!

Have you ever watched the fascinating interaction between a person
who is hearing impaired or deaf and a person who is hearing as they
try to communicate? The Chaplinesque antics are either painfully
awkward to watch or slapstick funny, depending on which person
you are, speaker or receiver, in the moving dialogue. It can be painful because of the awkward moves the hearing person has to make
in order to be understood by the person with the hearing impairment. Or it can be humorous when the person who is deaf or hearing impaired, not *wanting* to receive any communication from the
hearing person, shuts him or her out—humorous, that is, unless you
are the hearing person, sinking in a pool of exasperation.

I speak from the perspective of the hearing person, for I have
seen my father, who has two hearing aids, perform just such an act.
When my brother and I were small and my father was just becoming accustomed to his hearing aids, he soon discovered that he had
some control over our loudness. Whenever my brother and I entered a room my father was in, his hand would shoot up to his
hearing aids to turn down the volume. He was able to hear us only
perfectly well *without* the aid of any mechanical devices. My mother,
who knew full well the power game at play, would laugh to herself.

Henry Kisor, a journalist who is hearing impaired and lip reads
rather than using American Sign Language, tells a story that un-
derlines the importance of humor in interactions between those

with hearing impairments and those without. He writes about an incident that took place some years ago when he was suffering from a bout of intestinal flu. He was sitting in his living room reading a book when he suddenly broke wind. He writes:

> My elder son, Colin, then five years old, dashed in wide-eyed from the kitchen and inquired, "What's that big loud noise?"
>
> Mystified, I arose from the couch, peered out the window, and said, "*What* pig outdoors?"
>
> My son stared at me dumbfoundedly. What pig?
>
> Go ahead, look in the mirror and watch your lips: to a lip reader "What's that big loud noise?" looks exactly like "What's that pig outdoors?"[1]

The loss of any sense—hearing, sight, taste, or touch—poses an enormous challenge to any person. We live in a culture that assumes that "normal" people can hear, see, taste, and feel. Being deaf can open up a huge social chasm between those who "suffer" from such a disability and those who do not find themselves in such a predicament and do not understand. In the hearing world, deaf people tend to be taken for granted or ignored if they are lucky, lonely and rejected if they are not. That's why the eighteenth-century English lexicographer Samuel Johnson called deafness "the most desperate of human calamities."[2]

Of all our senses, hearing is the one that appears to be the hardest to train. In the eye, for example, there are muscles that allow one to zero in on a single thing. And certain practices can train the taste buds to more discriminating. But hearing is different. For the next few seconds, try to focus your hearing on just one sound, be it the rush of the air conditioner, the roar of road noise, or the shush of the ubiquitous white noise. Or, without putting your hands to your ears, try to block out the sound of my voice. It's nearly impossible to focus our hearing on a single sound and block out the extraneous noises. This makes even more miraculous the number of times we are accused of being hard of hearing or having "selective hearing," because, physiologically speaking, we do not have such a capacity.[3]

Being hearing impaired affects not only persons with the disability, but also those trying to communicate with him or her—the entire Christian community. Until the message I am trying to communicate is received by another person, I remain ignored, unseen—a persona non grata. A wall of silence is built and maintained. The act of being heard, of having one's message received, of being seen and recognized, validates a person as relevant to the discussion called life and others participating in it.

Deafness or hearing impairment is not only a physiological problem when it comes to matters of the Christian faith. One may have the ability to hear and still *not* hear the voice of the Word of God, Jesus Christ. For example, when Jesus told a parable, like the parable of the sower, he ended with the admonition "Let anyone with ears listen!" (Matt. 13:10). What is the implication? Not everyone who has ears, the ability to hear, will understand the parable. Even though the knowledge of God's dominion is revealed in such simple parables, there are many who, even with the ability to hear, simply do not comprehend what is being told. Some people choose to be deaf to the Word of God, whether or not they can hear it with their ears. They are truly disabled.

Such a disability can only be habilitated by recognizing that the gift of hearing of the Word of God, Jesus Christ, is made known in the context of Christian community. It is among God's people that we learn the practice of discerning the "voice" of God amid the cacophony of sounds in this world. It is in the church that we may follow the rhythmic "noise" of the Holy Spirit through the habits of Christian life together, laughing at the ways in which we are moving with God, and God with us, in this world.

This gift of hearing is further dramatized by Jesus in the illustrations he makes about sheep and the shepherd's voice in the Gospel of John. When Jesus is standing in the Temple at the time of the Festival of Dedication (when the Jewish people celebrated the reconstruction of the Temple once destroyed), Jesus makes startlingly clear to the Jewish authorities that Jesus and God the Father are one. They are not merely *like* each other, or *with* each other; they are *one* (John 10:30).

How do the disciples of Jesus know this? Because Jesus told them that "my sheep hear my voice, I know them, and they follow me" (John 10:27). We are chosen to hear this voice, metaphorically and literally speaking; to comprehend and be engaged by the presence of Christ in the Christian community. We are to be cradled by the good news that the "Word of God," Jesus, is able to reach beyond and crush the physiological barriers that deny some the ability to hear with human ears. As the shepherd gestures to his sheep to make their way to safer and greener pastures, using either words of mouth or "rod and staff," we are led by the presence of Christ to live in the hope-filled dominion of God.

To find ourselves in God's good pastures, in God's gracious company, is good news! Such good news is to be shared, for it is a gift that God has chosen to give us, God's community. Granted, there are some in the Christian community who literally cannot hear the Word of God, physiologically or spiritually speaking, but they are still members of this community. This is made possible because we are part of the greater gift—being a member of Christ's body, in which some may hear God for those who may not. The apostle Paul wrote that "if the whole body were an eye, where would the hearing be? If the whole body were hearing, where would the sense of smell be? But as it is, God arranged the members in the body, each one of them, as he chose" (1 Cor. 12:17–18).

In this body of Christ, the church, let us practice listening for and hearing God anew. The ways in which God's voice is heard must also be understood metaphorically, because God communicates with us, makes his will known, reveals the love of a shepherd for his sheep, in the most surprising ways. It takes practiced hearing to appreciate the marvelous ways in which God's Spirit communicates with us—in the voice of a child who loudly shouts or signs "Hosanna" while waving a palm branch in celebration of Jesus' journey into our lives, and in the stirring silence of prayer, when all is still but for the comforting knowledge that God is present. We need to point out for each other the ways God in Christ wants us to serve him by serving one another.

There is no easy recipe, no trick, for this kind of hearing. And one's auditory ability need not be at maximum strength. Fear not, those of you who are deaf or hard of hearing. The God who hears us also speaks to us in ways that may use human language. But

God's message also also reaches us in ways no mortal ingenuity can comprehend. The God who receives us is now beckoning to us by using hands that are masters of sign language and hearing aids that sharpen muffled hearing. God is beckoning to us with embracing hugs, caring gestures, kind words—beckoning us to come in thanksgiving for this gift of life and love, and love of life in Jesus Christ.

chapter five

make way for electric-blue wheelchairs!

Have you ever considered how pragmatic, how utilitarian, how user-friendly the church is? Despite countless sermons denouncing such notions, many congregations still promote the idea that the value of going to church lies solely in what we *do* in the name of God in the busyness of congregational life, rather than *being* in God. We reinforce this with ostentatious displays honoring those who *do* the most in the church. Just like other volunteer groups, we give plaques, award dinners, even monetary gifts for tangible tasks completed by parishioners. Then even more work is piled merrily on those who *do* the most voluntary work, forgetting the presence of the silent others in the life of the church. Behaviorists call this work-and-reward system "positive reinforcement," and for them it works. When these people become burned out on church life, a crusade to find others to fill their vacated positions begins.

The problem with this work-and-reward view of church life is that it doesn't fit with Christ's understanding of the workings of God's dominion. For example, consider the importance of merely *being* a child of God's, as illustrated by this story of Jenny.[1] Jenny is a shy six-year-old who attends a Presbyterian church where I was the interim pastor. She stands out from the other young children in her church because she has cerebral palsy, which affects her speech and all four of her limbs, causing them to move in wild arcs when she is surprised. She communicates verbally when she can control the complex muscles that let her talk. She is also learning how to use a head stick, which allows her to communicate by pointing to figures on a computer keyboard.

What really attracts the other children in the church to Jenny is her wheelchair, an eye-catching electric-blue outfit specially molded for Jenny's contorted physique. It looks more like something to blast off into space in than to wheel around within the sanctuary. Jenny is truly beloved when she takes off down the ramps and sidewalks around the church, giving the other children rides. She screams in wild abandon as the children take turns holding on for dear life, hoping not to fall off around the turns. Jenny smiles as broadly as humanly possible, knowing she is a hit.

But there is more to Jenny's story than her wheelchair. Jenny's family is poor. She lives with her mother and two siblings, and no father. Her mother depends on the financial support of government agencies, as well as the church toward the end of some months. Because there is so little money coming in, the family rides around in an old Datsun station wagon, and Jenny's mother has to wrestle with the wheelchair for a good five minutes to get Jenny inside the car. As Jenny grows, this transportation mode is becoming critical. It has also became a Godsend of an issue for this church.

Last January, the pastor in Jenny's church died, and his death exacerbated alarming divisions within the church. Groups around the church divided themselves into strange, balkanized zones. Each group had little in common with the others, and each group was sustained by a common bitterness toward the others. Some people were struggling against the very theological integrity of the church to the point of questioning whether it whould remain within the jurisdiction of the Presbyterian Church (U.S.A.).

Jenny's transportation problem was a divine miracle, because it provided an opportunity for these otherwise fractious, divided camps to join together in a common cause—getting Jenny's family a van, which would cost about $15,000. To plan how to raise the money, the groups had to communicate with one another. And that's where the miracle happened.

One hot, humid August weekend, the church held a baseball tournament. There were two teams from this Presbyterian church and one team from each of two neighboring churches. The use of the fields, food for the concessions, and public address system were all donated, and the umpires and game announcer volunteered their time. By the time the tournament ended, $13,000 had been raised from the sale of tickets and food from the concessions. But something more important than fundraising had taken place. People from the contentious groups had not only laughed and played with one another—they had put their differences aside in the name of Jenny, one of God's children.

Jenny is one of God's children, and she is an integral part of this Christian community. And because of her family's great need, Jenny's very presence in this church provided a much-needed excuse for people who had once been divided to come together in a common cause.

This simple story reveals the untruths that are sustained among many Christians regarding the role—and the very presence—of people with disabilities in the church. A great many people with developmental, emotional, or physical disabilities have been kept out of the church, because a great many people who appear "normal" misunderstand the church. Families with and advocates for people with disabilities are often asked by church leaders "What can they *do* in church?" or "What will they *get* out of it?" Some church leaders think of the church and God in pragmatic terms: You can only be a part of this exclusive club if you can *do* something, and you can't *get* something by doing nothing.

When our value in the church is reduced, simplified, and categorized by what we can *do* in the church, the church is in danger. This misunderstanding shows that we no longer remember that, without God, we are nothing. We have been fooled into thinking that if we simply *do* the things of the church, we may find favor with God. Because people with disabilities are not able to do certain things in church, and because they don't appear to fit a narrow image of a "normal" God, their value is questioned in churches, especially those who are severely or profoundly disabled. This draconian measure of worth is contrary to Jesus' teaching. Recognizing that we are created in the image of God, we are called to surrender all we have to Christ and live in total dependence upon the graciousness of the Creator. Jesus kept pointing out to the disciples that, regardless of our brilliant abilities or our visible limitations, in the presence of God, we are all disabled, handicapped, and crippled by sin. Our salvation came by Jesus' death upon the cross and resurrection three days later. It made us dependent upon being saved by God in Christ, who alone admits us to full participation in the dominion of God. We are God's own children, and God alone chooses what to do with us.

This is the point of Jesus' parable of the laborers in the vineyard (Matt. 20:1–16). Those who came early in the day and were glad to work were not complaining about what *they* received from the master; they were greatly disturbed by how much the *others* received. In their understanding of earthly justice, those who came last and did less should receive less than those who came early and worked all day. Their reward is a caustic remark: "Take your pay and go."

The implications of this parable are evident. Those who came early and questioned the very judgment of the master are like those who try to turn God's gift of faith into a legal contract bound by the ultimatum: "If I do this amount of work for God and the church, for this period of time, then I deserve God's grace." They demand that God should operate according to their ideas of "equal justice" and fair pay. They fail to understand that living in Christ means living a life where grace is never a bounty to be earned. Grace is God's gift of love freely given, which we don't deserve but which we, with humble gratitude, receive.

We worship the God of Creation as God's creatures, dependent upon God's gift of grace. God chooses to be generous in loving us. The bounteous, gracious, efficacious power of God's mercy is what happens upon a people in worshipful prayer. Our creaturely abilities and limitations are no barriers to such penetrating, ever-present, Godly love.

That is why Jenny and her family come to church—to be among God's people in worshiping God through song and word, deed and prayer. Jenny's very presence in the electric-blue wheelchair, her transportation crisis, and the limitations brought about by her disabilities have blessed many people with a miraculous insight—

that our worth is not found in what we do, but in Christ's body. In Christ's body, we realize whose we are. We are God's children, God's own. And we need to make way for girls in electric-blue wheelchairs. Because Jenny is who she is, she has enabled this once bitterly divided congregation to start upon the path of healing and wholeness. God has chosen to be generous with us all.

chapter six

the abilities disabilities make possible

The naturalist Annie Dillard paints a provocative portrait of expectations when God's people gather in response to the call of the Almighty to worship. In *Teaching a Stone to Talk*, Dillard shocks us by exhorting church ushers to pass out life preservers and crash helmets to parishioners as we pray for God's presence in our midst, for a dramatic transformation is not far behind when we wake "the sleeping god."[1] But transformation need not be so violently dramatic. God often chooses to discomfort us and transform our lives quietly, perhaps by way of a seldom-used side door that we never expected to find open.

In just such way, God has transformed my perception of what it means to be human in the context of the church of Jesus Christ. No longer do I see those people whom society has labeled "disabled" as any *more* limited or *more* able than anyone else in the context of the Christian church. Instead, I see Rachel, a four-year-old red-headed girl who is learning to control her legs and arms and voice. She is beginning to sing in her own way whenever she hears the pianist in her father's country Presbyterian church bang out the opening hymn on Sunday morning. I sit near Burt, who is listening to the sermon, singing hymns, and practicing the ritualistic gestures of worship. Burt is a young man with a hot temper and repetitive muscular behavior that some people believe is beyond his control. But in the context of an Episcopal worship service, his muscles are controlled by the template of ritualistic gestures of worshiping God. Burt is transfixed by the graceful gestures of the Christian faith.

Rachel and Burt have two things in common. First, inside the context of their respective Christian congregations, they are both Christians who are worshiping God. And second, outside the context of the Christian church, society has constructed labels and categories for them in order to explain who they are and why they act the way they do or describe their moral status given their disability. For example, consider this poem by Miller Williams about babies born with disabilities:

The Ones That Are Thrown Out

One has flippers. This one is like a seal.
One has gills. This one is like a fish.
One has webbed hands, is like a duck.
One has a little tail, is like a pig.
One is like a frog
with no dome at all above the eyes.

They call them bad babies.

They didn't mean to be bad
but who does.[2]

Society's labels and categories have kept many people with disabilities outside the doors of the church. Rachel, who has been labeled with "mental retardation" and "cerebral palsy," and Burt, who has "Tourette's syndrome," would not be allowed in many churches. The sole reason for this exclusion is that their particular limitations have been labeled and categorized. Many churches see the labels first and don't believe that they—the "disabled"—can understand what happens in church, especially during worship.

Labels and categories used for identifying our human limitations were not always intended to pigeonhole people for life. In the nineteenth century, the French educator Alfred Binet was called upon by the French government to develop a technique for identifying children whose lack of academic success might suggest a need for some form of remedial education. Today we call this test an "I.Q.," or "intelligence quotient," test. The scientist Stephen Jay Gould wrote that the scores from these tests were intended to be used for the practical purpose of identifying those children in need of help, not for marking children as innately incapable or ranking normal children.[3]

Disabilities are inevitable human phenomena that have existed since the beginning of human time, and they will always be a part of humankind, because to be human is to be mortal and fallible. There have always been, and will always be, people with specific limitations in thinking and feeling, in the use of their physical bodies or their medical condition, and in the coordination of their senses. To understand the nature of these given, universal human limitations, society has constructed definitions, labels, and categories to try and describe and explain why and what a person can and cannot do. All labels and categories—from "mental retardation" to "blindness"—are socially constructed, cultural concoctions; therefore, they directly reflect what a society considers valuable or worthy of serious concern.

As societies change in terms of what they value or how they view particular phenomena, the labels and categories change as well. For example, people with marked intellectual limitations were called "feeble minded" at the beginning of the twentieth century. As we enter the twenty-first century, we call such a person either "mentally retarded" or "developmentally delayed." For example, since 1921, there have been nine revisions to the definition of mental retardation in America, and other countries have their own definitions of this condition. These changing definitions reflect the underlying philosophical ideals of the Enlightenment, in which the mind—the source of rational, logical thinking—is central to understanding and promoting progress in the world. Philosophy students learn early on René Descartes' axiom, "I think, therefore I am." And if one cannot think as others do, then how is one's existence to be understood? Reason, according to philosopher Immanuel Kant, assures "man's release from his self-imposed tutelage," a tutelage encouraged by the church.

The church has acted strangely by not challenging society's definitions, labels, and categories for the human condition. It has embraced and used society's labels with little if any critical reflection about what it was embracing—namely, the ideals of the Enlightenment. In doing so, it reaffirms the norms society has constructed for human behavior.

The use of one's mind is central to the worship of God. Many congregations and parishes, especially Protestant churches, have repeatedly told people with mental retardation (or their families) that they probably should not come to their church because they wouldn't understand the sermon, which is central to their understanding of worship. Because of the centrality of the written and spoken word in Protestant worship, people with a variety of limitations often feel ostracized by these practices of worship. The little girl who is not able to hear, the old man with poor eyesight, the young man with cerebral palsy whose speech is hard to understand until you grasp its rhythm—none of these people are able to worship God in the same ways others are in these Protestant liturgies, so they are not welcomed to participate in worship of God. For many people in our churches, the goal of worship has become proving the existence of God with the faculty of the mind, rather than worshipping God with one's body, mind, and spirit.

This was not always the case for the church. Up until the Enlightenment, people lived in a society comprised of a complex network of reciprocal rights and duties. It was taken for granted that creation in general and in human relations in particular had a divine purpose. There were no random acts in the world: God was the center of all life, and there was an inevitable end toward which all of human history was moving—toward the dominion of God.

Before the many manifestations of the Protestant Reformation, (a movement in the life of the church later reinforced by Enlightenment developments), one "knew" God in and by life in the church. God's presence was made known by and experienced through faith by grace, and this was facilitated by the complex symbols and purposeful gestures and rituals of the church. Churches were filled with sacred images in sculptures and stained-glass windows; the very architecture of the Gothic cathedral was a symbol of the cross of Christ. After the Reformation, the church began to resemble a lecture hall with a minister leading the service. The pulpit was moved from the side of the church and placed front and center. Altars were replaced by simple tables, and the once-important gestures of faith and devotion, such as kneeling for prayers and using one's hands, for example, were replaced by worshipers sitting still and listening, using their rational minds to understand a reasoning God. In many ways, the church is held captive by the very ideals of the Enlightenment.

This captivity is unnecessary. The church is not bound by the surrounding world's definitions of what is or isn't normal in light of the Enlightenment. The church is in itself a culture unique among other cultures, a culture where people are welcomed not because of what they can or cannot do, but because of whose they are—God's children. Christianity is a culture that produces and re-pro-duces itself by the people who are called to be the body of Christ. It is an ordering of life that locates people in Christian community by certain essential practices, such as prayer and worship, that re-veals not only what is the good we share in common, that is, God; it also embodies its telos, namely, the dominion of God. Christian-ity in general, and the congregation or parish in particular, needs to understand itself as a culture that practices specific faithful ges-tures that the world finds peculiar, to say the least.

In the church, we readily acknowledge that a person is more than his or her score on a standardized test. We understand that all human life is a gift given by the Creator God. In Genesis 1:27, we read that all human beings were created in the image of God. We have life because God loved us into creation, forming us "from the dust of the ground" (Gen. 2:7), and breathed into us the breath of life. This proclamation of our beginnings as a human race is essen-tial for clarifying how the Christian community understands hu-man life: as a gift.

In life, God continually reminds us that we are valued for who and whose we are, and not necessarily for our outward actions. Consider Samuel the Judge, searching for the one who will replace King Saul. God has chosen a successor and sends Samuel to find this person among the children of Jesse in the town of Bethlehem. In the search process, Samuel looks at the outer shells of people, but God is looking elsewhere: "Do not look on his appearance or on the height of his stature, because I have rejected him; for God does not see as mortals see; they look on outward appearance, but God looks on the heart" (1 Sam. 16:7). Nowhere in Scripture is a person praised or rejected for physical, mental, or emotional abilities or limitations. God looks instead upon the heart, which is often used as a synonym for a person's character.

The apostle Paul reminds us that, in a society that bellows about the rights of individuals as autonomous, disconnected entities with certain inalienable rights, our primary community, the church, should be considered one body—Christ's body—in which we are all individual members (Rom. 12:3–8). All people have been born into this body, with certain, specific gifts and talents that are necessary for the health of the body of Christ. Paul goes so far as to chastise those who label certain members of the body more important than others. In *this* body—Christ's body—those parts considered weaker are not dispensable, but rather indispensable, and those who appear less honorable are truly more honorable (1 Cor. 12:22–24). Each person, endowed with God's grace, is born into this one body with distinctive members.

For Christians, Christ's body—not the world—is our primary community, our culture not of choice but of calling. In *Resident Aliens*, theologians Stanley Hauerwas and Will Willimon argue rightly that the church, understood "as those called out by God, embodies a social alternative that the world cannot on its own terms know." The church is a "colony of resident aliens," living by different virtues from those of the surrounding society, because the church is embedded in God's story, which leads us toward God's dominion, a commonwealth of agape.[4]

As a social alternative, a community of resistance, the church as body embraces the diversity of skills and talents, of being and becoming, that is naturally found within Christ. Again, Paul is clear that the body is not one massive foot or hand, one big eye or ear. Instead, God has arranged the members in the body, each one of them, as God chooses.

In recent years, many deaf people have declared that deafness is no longer a "disability," but rather a culture as distinct as African

American culture or a Native American culture. Many deaf people have left the church of the hearing, for they felt it held no place for or appreciation of those who cannot hear as others do. In response, they have created their own congregations for the deaf within various denominations. This is nothing new when you consider that institutions for people with mental retardation have had separate worship services since at least the nineteenth century.

The existence of such churches, whose sole criterion for membership is a physical or sensory limitation, is the result of a broken church. These separate churches-within-churches have embraced the ideals and divisions of the world. They have failed to comprehend that the church is different from all other human gatherings in the world. It serves and worships a different God. Both types of churches—those exclusively for people with disabilities and those who exclude people with disabilities—have failed. They have failed to dream of possibilities and imagine ways for all members of Christ's body to be welcomed together as one.

Another way to understand the nature of the church is to reclaim the vision that the social strategies, objectives, and aims of the church are—because of our faith in God in Christ—distinctly different from those of the surrounding secular society.

First, we must accept the fact that the church views the human condition differently from society at large. God understands perfectly well that all humans are disabled, crippled, impaired, and handicapped by the evil of sin, no matter what their mental, emotional, or physical abilities or limitations. No one is perfect, good, or faithful except God. Whether one is in a wheelchair or walks upright, uses braille or sees with twenty-twenty vision, blurts and mumbles through the hymns or sings with unwavering voice, God is looking beyond these outer shells and uncontrollable actions. God focuses instead on what is important, on the matters that weigh heavily upon our hearts, our characters. In the church, we all are present before the One who sees us for who we are, and yet loves us still.

Second, we are all dependent upon God in Christ for the gift of grace which alone saves the church from its own mutually agreed-upon pattern of self-destruction. By telling the disciples to let the children gather round, Jesus points out to us that we, like children, are ultimately dependent upon the love of God. Hauerwas and Willimon rightly point out that this is the odd nature of God's dominion, this idea of sustaining a loving, caring, faithful, and hopeful dependence upon God for our very being. No one is independent of God. All of us are utterly dependent upon God for the very food we eat and the very breath we breathe.

This transforming perception of our shared dependence upon God came most clearly into focus in church—as I listened to the story of Rachel learning to sing the opening hymn with the congregation, and as I opened my hands for the broken bread next to Burt, expecting to control his actions while the act of worship did it for me. As I sat and ate, watched and listened, I caught a glimpse of a new vision of the indomitable power of God, present in the act of worship. It is in the company of sisters and brothers who, like me, were no longer disabled by sin, but forgiven by the redeeming love of Jesus Christ.

Part two

❦

The Church as Sanctuary

chapter seven

the spiritual abuse of people with disabilities

At that time the disciples came to Jesus and asked, "Who is the greatest in . . . heaven?" He called a child, whom he put among them, and said, "Truly I tell you, unless you change and become like children, you will never enter . . . heaven. Whoever becomes humble like this child is the greatest in . . . heaven. Whoever welcomes one such child in my name welcomes me.

"If any of you put a stumbling block before one of these little ones who believe in me, it would be better for you if a great millstone were fastened around your neck and you were drowned in the depth of the sea. Woe to the world because of stumbling blocks! Occasions for stumbling are bound to come, but woe to the one by whom the stumbling block comes!"

—Matt. 18:1–7

A scandal is occurring in American society. An injustice is being perpetrated in the church that few know is occurring and even fewer can respond to, because there is no language to talk about it. The scandalous injustice concerns the spiritual abuse of people with disabilities. The ones most wounded by this abuse are those society has defined as "disabled," whether it's the young boy with autism, the older woman with schizophrenia, the infant with Down's syndrome, or the young woman with Tourette's syndrome. Those who are guilty of carrying out the injustice, knowingly or unknowingly, are society in general and the church in particular.

Spiritual abuse comes in many forms. In one church, after a chorus of people with mental retardation sang the anthem for Sunday morning worship, the pastor began talking about angels. He started by talking about the angels in the Bible—the angel who wrestled with Jacob and the angels who sang "Gloria," announcing the birth of Jesus. Then he compared the sometimes sweet, frequently off-key sound of the present chorus of people with mental retardation as being a contemporary "sound of angels." But by labeling them as angels, he inadvertently robbed them of the richness of being human and left them with the barrenness of one-dimensional, postcard innocence.

Some may regard a person with mental retardation as angelic, but some others view a person with disabilities as demonic or somehow the product of sin. While health-service providers understand the root causes of mental retardation and physical, emotional, and behavioral disabilities as physiological or social in nature, this is not true for some churches. When I was the Director of Religious Life at an institution for children with severe emotional, behavioral, and developmental disabilities, I heard stories from children and parents alike about the roots of the children's disabling conditions: Satan. Many familes (and children themselves) believed that their lack of control was attributable to demonic possession. To back up such allegations, these people would point to signs and symbols visible on the children's units. Even though the children were not allowed to listen to heavy metal music or wear T-shirts with skulls, pentagrams, or upside-down crosses, they hummed the tunes and freely drew such pictures when staff members gave them pens or pencils. More than once I was approached by staff members about the possibility of calling in a Roman Catholic priest to perform an exorcism.

The third type of spiritual abuse is perpetrated by government agencies that provide support for people with disabilities and their families. People who work in such agencies may not intentionally deprive those with disabilities of the opportunity to go to church or synagogue, but there is an oft-repeated line about "separation of church and state." A woman who is a state coordinator for services for people with retardation recently outlined for me that state's innovative program of community-based programs for these people. This woman, who is a Christian, completely left congregations and parishes out of the formula for this so-called community-based program.

There is an accepted absence of spirituality in private institutions that care for the health of people with mental retardation or mental illness and children with emotional or behavioral disorders. Unless a particular program happened to be founded by a religious order, communities of Christian faith are generally shut out. Most institutions, especially those established in recent decades, purport to offer "holistic" care, and yet they do not include spirituality in their programs in any meaningful way. Some might allow a chaplain to come in once or twice a week to lead worship or Bible study, but this token gesture is overshadowed by the omnipresent, pragmatic "religion of psychology," especially behaviorism and psychotherapy. One behavioral psychologist told me: "You and I serve a different god. We are reading from different scriptures, different stories. My faith is in the religion of behaviorism while yours is in Jesus Christ. . . . We believe in different things."

Given the Christian belief that a human being is a unity of body, mind, and spirit incorporated in Christ, dependent upon other human beings and, more important, God, these examples qualify as spiritual abuse not because the link between body and mind is being ignored, but because the issues of spirit and community are being denied. Whether we romanticize retardation, demonize a child with an emotional disability, or flatly deny the spiritual needs of those who are disabled, we compromise or denigrate the humanity of that individual. As a result, those with disabling conditions are sometimes treated as non-persons. They are viewed as nothing more than their conditions, objects to be venerated or exorcised by the church or manipulated by secular health professionals.

The denial of the spirit by health professionals is often motivated by a desire to keep treatment plans simple and predictable. To view a person as an individual, a child of God, might profoundly complicate an already overburdened system. Recognizing the spiritual needs of disabled persons makes the task of professional care far more complex.

In order to stop this type of spiritual abuse, the church needs to broaden its long-discussed theological rationalizations about the human condition to include all people. Adopting this theological perspective means focusing on the human condition: to be human, Christians believe, is to acknowledge our imperfection and vulnerability. Thinking theologically about those people many dismiss as "disabled" is to see and hear one another for who, and whose, we really are—God's children. To acknowledge that one is a child of God is to understand more fully the human condition as the rich combination of mind, body, *and* spirit—as is articulated in Scripture, understood by faith, retold in the church's creeds, and celebrated in the liturgy.

Theologians concur that human life is a creation of God the Creator (Gen. 1:27), a gift given by the Creator and not of our own making or choosing. Theologians also commonly agree that, being created in the image of God, human beings have been endowed with the gift of creativity as well as the ability to make choices within the finite limits of the garden. As the story of creation unfolds, we are painfully aware of the sinful, willful choices made by human creatures that knocked out of balance the once-harmonious relationship between Creator, creature, and creation.

In reflecting upon this turn of events in the creation story, it is apparent that turmoil is now part of the human condition. The female human experiences pain in bringing forth children (Gen. 3:16). People must toil for their food (Gen. 3:18). And to remind us of our mortality, we read that we are creatures of dust and "to dust . . . shall return" (Gen. 3:19). Because of our human arrogance in questioning God's commands, we live a limited, disabled, handicapped life as creatures of earthly dust.

But this is only the beginning of the story. Many events of life that began in the creation stories continue after the dismissal of human creatures from the shelter of God's garden. To begin with, God has been and still is with us. While we turned our backs on God, God did not turn against creation. God has not left us; we are the ones who attempted to leave God.

According to the story, there is still the relationship women and men have with one another. God created us as contingent beings, to be in relationship with others as God is in relationship with creation. Just as creatures are dependent upon God for their being, participants of community are dependent upon one another to meet their material, emotional, spiritual needs. The Christian community is not a holding area where we passively wait for the dominion of God. It is here, in this Christian community, where human beings learn how sinfulness has deeply compromised our condition. In the hymn "Come Thou Fount of Every Blessing" is the line "prone to wander, Lord I feel it, prone to leave the God I love." This is sin—being "naturally" prone to wander *away* from God and the things of God.

But sin is not all we learn about in the Christian community. We also learn about God's gift of grace and love for a people naturally insecure and weary from life's labor. Christians are taught to depend on the gifts of the God's grace, Christ's atoning love, and the Holy Spirit's peace. It is in the Christian community that people know they are called by God to live life as obedient people, as Christ's disciples always in need of God's gracious love. And it is God's Spirit who is still forming the body of Christ on earth, always with an eye on the dominion of God.

There is nothing new in this theological confession. It is straight talk for a Presbyterian Christian. However, this description of human beings as sinful, dependent beings in need of God's gift of grace should make it inescapably clear for *all* of us that one's mental, physical, or sensory condition is neither a help nor a hindrance in relationship to God. Because humans cannot save themselves by their own works, only by receiving the gift of God's grace, then what my physical, mental, or emotional condition does or does not allow me to do is irrelevant in the context of the Christian community. Because one's limitations are neither a help nor a hindrance in relationship with God in Christ, one must make the contributions one can in sharing our God-given gifts and talents in Christ's body. Although society—and the church—have labeled people either "able" or "disabled," God has a different idea of the human condition. In God's eyes, no one is created as either an angel or a devil. All have sinned. All fall short of God's glory. And all are saved by God's grace.

The implication of this Christian "straight talk" is that disabled people are, in the Christian community, as much in need of instruction about their natural state of sinful rebellion as anyone else in the church. One is not more *or* less a creature of sin than anyone else by virtue of a disabling condition.

Because of this implication, people whom society has labeled "disabled," like any other parishioner, are *also* dependent upon God's gift of gracious love in the sacraments of baptism and eucharist. In Christ's community, living out the ongoing narrative of God's jealous love for this creation and the promise of the dominion of God, Christ's people are united.

Dependence may put a crimp in the federal government's Americans with Disabilities Act, which is advocating for the *in*dependence of people labeled "disabled." Much of what is written in this legislation is a product of an ethos that praises rugged individualism and scorns dependent community life. Consider the story of a married couple in Michigan, both of whom had cerebral palsy, who had a baby. The issue before the state of Michigan was this: should people with disabilities such as cerebral palsy be allowed to have babies? The concern was that they could not "independently" care for a baby and would need the services of the state in order to raise her. The underlying message in this case was that only independent, "healthy" people should be allowed to have children. No mention was made of other sources of care (a congregation, friends, an extended family), nor of that most important attribute of all parents—love, the adoring love that shone in the eyes and in the awkward-looking yet obviously caring gestures of the couple.

The place and time to work on correcting the dehumanization of people with disabilities, to be serious about being human, as creatures created in God's image, to teach people about the reality of sin and the gift of God's grace, is in the church—*now*. Many times a person with disabilites comes as a stranger into the midst of such a community life. As a stranger, he or she expands the imaginations of congregants and parishioners, opening up for them the very breadth of beautiful variance in God's act of creating us human.

The powerful presence of the stranger in Christian communities continually challenges us to look for God in the face of the unexpected as well as the known. I have been witness in Christian communities to many transforming events that were fostered by Christ's Spirit in the presence and participation of the "disabled." Consider, for example, what happened in one congregation when a group of friends from a British l'Arche community (a Catholic community for and with adults with mental retardation) could not be "controlled" during the installation of a Catholic priest in a new church. The service had already begun and, according to the priest waiting to be installed, the procession was overly solemn. Suddenly, exploding through the doors came members of a l'Arche house that the priest had lived in. As the house members talked to and hugged parishioners on their way down the center aisle, they brought with them laughter, smiles, and a spirit of Christlike celebration that had been sorely missing. Strangers who are hospitable to us force us to look at our own callousness and inhospitality.

In the same l'Arche community lived a woman named Rose. Rose was eccentric—full of confusing clutter in her room, and often confused about life in general. Yet Rose taught Jon, a college student I had brought to live in the community, about the gift of giving. The first time Jon met Rose, she reached into the shopping bag that was always by her side, the bag that contained all her earthly possessions. She pulled out a mug and gave it to Jon, saying, "This is for you." Then she left abruptly. Not sure how to receive this gift, Jon quietly returned it to her room. He didn't know how to accept the gift of another person *he* deemed to be worse off than himself. He later found out that Rose had been hurt by his refusal of the gift.

The most interesting thing about strangers in community is the transformation of strangers into friends. Once invited and brought into the Christian community, a newcomer is no longer a stranger. This does not mean that such a person is no longer important to the community, but no longer is he or she a potent catalyst of change. There is always a fresh need for the stranger in the Christian community, not so the community population can grow larger numerically, but rather so it can grow into a fuller appreciation for the ways of God.

It is fascinating that in some l'Arche communities, when there is an opening for a person with a disability, one who is especially disabled is chosen. Communities invite this person to come and live with them because not only will the person with a disability find care, but learning how to care anew in Christ's spirit stretches the other members. The mysterious paradox is that, by welcoming strangers, those whom we consider among "the least" of our brothers and sisters, we are welcoming Christ (Matt. 25:40).

Spiritual abuse is the act of denying people considered "disabled" their full humanity. It is treating and caring for them as if they were less than human. All people in the church who want to be in the community of Christ should be welcomed into this fragile gathering of hidden saints and needy sinners. All those gathered together in the name of Christ do so out of dependence upon the gift of salvation found only in this storied community. To *not* welcome those whom Jesus considered the "little ones," like children—no matter how young or old we are as God's children—like those considered to be "disabled" in society, so ready and open to receiving the reign of God, brings terrible consequences: "It would be better for you if a great millstone were fastened around your neck and you were drowned in the depth of the sea," says Jesus (Matt. 18:6).

The choice, as always, is ours to make.

chapter eight

let the little children
come to me

The Importance of Children
with Disabilities in the Church

People were bringing little children to him in order that he might touch them; and the disciples spoke sternly to them. But when Jesus saw this, he was indignant and said to them, "Let the little children come to me; do not stop them; for it is to such as these that the realm of God belongs. Truly I tell you, whoever does not receive the realm of God as a little child will never enter it." And he took them up in his arms, laid his hands on them, and blessed them.

—Mark 10:13–16

For two years my life was filled, if not crowded, with children who have emotional, behavioral, or developmental disabilities. I served as Director of Religious Life in a secular, private psychiatric facility for more than one hundred children from around the country. I am still intellectually, emotionally, and spiritually consumed by the questions their very presence raises about life in general, and about God in particular. They called me their Spiritual Dude. To them, I was an explicit "religious" presence. My work there became a unique way of entering into the lives of these assorted "saints" and "sinners."

Children labeled as having emotional or behavioral disabilities are often not able to navigate the rough, angry conditions of their lives. In response to cancerous family relationships, estrangement from gangs or other peer groups, and frustration with the unpredictable nature of life in general, these children struggle to extract meaning from chaos. They stand ready to destroy all that stands in their way. Viewing these children in context helps us fathom the uncontrollable rage of a boy who is about to hurl a mahogany chair at a staff member because his father just called to say he wouldn't be visiting this weekend as planned—for the seventh weekend in a row. It helps soften our judgment of the suicidal adolescent who keeps taking little bites of flesh out of her arms because it "just feels good." It enables us to understand the depressed, tormented adolescent who sexually molested his sister, after having been first molested by his mother at age four. It allows us to feel compassion for the lonely, frightened, hyperactive child who has been in six therapeutic foster homes, but keeps running in search of the home of her memories from a time before her parents were sent to prison for drug possession.

I learned additional lessons about the politics of institutional life, the bondage of being labeled "disabled," and remarkable faith in God from four Christian storytellers: Steve,[1] who is white, sixteen years old, and from a rural area in the South; Randy, who is white, thirteen, and originally from a large northern city; Dennis, who is a fourteen-year-old Hispanic American from a large southern city; and Stephanie, seventeen, who is African American and from a large city in a mid-Atlantic state.

Steve boldly proclaims that he is a Christian in a group of other adolescents and staff. Tall and broad, Steve is a gentle giant. He has several earrings in one ear and blonde hair cut close to his scalp in the back but hanging in his eyes in the front. Steve had been at a fundamentalist Christian camp for adolescent boys with emotional problems until he was kicked out: "I went against God's will and I went against their standards. I came back drunk a couple of times, and I cursed out one of the dorm parents."

Steve is in search of community—a place where he can settle down and grow. He has been in and out of his family's home since he was nine. The longest period he has spent with his family since he was nine is three months, "and then they would zip me back into another hospital, or I'd do something to deserve it. But now I'm working hard, and I believe that God's behind me. And I just got news today that I will be leaving in one month if I keep going straight." He has no desire to go home to—or to be in touch at all with—his grandmother, mother, stepbrother, or stepsister. He doesn't like living with them, a point he has made clear by torturing their animals and burning down their home.

Even with this history, Steve believes in Christ, and he believes that our sins will be forgiven. "So that you'll be able to go to heaven when it all ends," he says. He experiences God as a shadow who hangs over his shoulders, though Satan is on one shoulder. "But God has more power, and he's over both of them, and he's directing me," Steve says.

When he thinks of Jesus, Steve first thinks of blood, because he views Jesus as "a sacrifice. I see Jesus' blood." Steve understands the mystery of Christ's act of atonement—"so that all men could live under God and believe in salvation and come live with him at the time of their death." He also understands Jesus as a heart: "I see him knocking and a lot of people resist, and that's where they mess up. Once you open that door, your life will turn around, and your life will not be gory. Once you have Jesus in your heart, you have someone."

Like Steve, Randy has found God, but not necessarily knocking at the door of his heart. Randy is also estranged from his family, in which he witnessed sexual abuse. He has a history of learning difficulties, possible developmental disabilities, and some behavioral problems. Randy's experience of God is most like the Bible's story of Joseph. Someone somewhere gave Randy an adaptation of Joseph's story that he could readily relate to. To Randy, Joseph's story is *his* story. Like Joseph, who had a loving relationship with his father, Randy grew up in a family that loved him. Also like Joseph, who was thrown out of his family, Randy has been displaced. And like Joseph, whose family found him in Egypt, remnants of Randy's family have recently shown interest in him.

Randy was the one who brought the Joseph story to my attention. After I had been telling some Bible stories on the unit, Randy came up and asked if we could read this beat-up book he had about Joseph and the multicolored coat. Surprised by his excitement for the story, I readily agreed. Once a week, we met in my office.

Sitting in my rocking chair, Randy would read a page, then I would read a page, finishing a chapter or two a week. Because he had problems reading, he stumbled over many of the words, but he persevered.

In our last session together, we discussed the moral of the story, which Randy summarized: "Even though you're jealous of somebody else [like your brothers], don't get jealous." To Randy, this is a story of jealousy among brothers, and our jealousy arises when we "don't have the stuff other people have." What is God's point to Joseph's story? "You should ask before you steal." In this regard, Randy feels that Joseph's story is a tale of good manners among people, especially in a family. Who is the hero of the story? "Joseph," he replies, with a smile on his face.

While Randy finds God in Bible stories, Dennis's experiences of God are more earthbound. One day, while talking about the animals we've had in our respective families, I asked if Jesus was a "cat man," to which Dennis replied, "No, he had a big dog . . . and the angels kept it." Why did God make dogs? "To protect people . . . to have a friend when someone dies, a best friend."

Dennis has a dog at home, or at least he talks as if there *is* a dog at home. He used to live with his mother, who worked full-time, but no father. He is in the institution because of "behavioral problems": he hustled drugs and was a courier of sorts for a gang in his home city. It was a way of life, a way of making money, and a way of being identified with a community since his family wasn't together.

Dennis has some firm ideas that show great understanding about the church and God's creation. I asked him once what it takes to have a church. "People," he replied. According to Dennis, we should all get together and be at peace with one another. "Everybody," he said. "But it's not going to happen . . . because of all these dumb people." Or in another discussion, I asked Dennis why he was created by God. "To draw and ride bikes . . . swimming fast."

One day Dennis might display a sure-footed faith in God; the next day, he isn't so sure what he believes. In one discussion, we talked about Christmas and what it meant for him. "Care, love . . . giving," he said. I asked Dennis if Christmas is an important time for him, and he quickly replied, "It's the most important time . . . [because] Jesus is born then." Then I asked him if he knew Jesus, and he answered, "I don't know him." Nor did Dennis know God or the Holy Spirit. I asked him if he wanted to know God, and he replied: "I do, but I don't know." Doubtful about his understanding of Jesus, I asked Dennis to clarify what he meant: "I don't know Jesus . . . I *believe* in Jesus. You know me. You see me. You hear me. I don't hear God. I don't see him. I believe in Jesus." I then asked Dennis how, if he couldn't see Jesus, he knew there was a Jesus to have faith in. "I believe in Jesus," he said, with conviction in his voice. Dennis believes in Jesus, whom he hasn't seen in person. The writer of Hebrews wrote: "[Faith is] the conviction of things not seen" (Heb. 11:1).

The final storyteller is Stephanie. Like many other young people at the hospital, Stephanie is a creative artist.She likes to dance, draw, write poetry, and act, and occasionally she likes to get attention from the staff or her boyfriend on the unit by faking a seizure. In one of my sessions with Stephanie, she was in an artistic mood and agreed to draw a picture of God for me. As she drew, she also shared her ideas on the very nature of our relationship to God.

"God has a beard," she began, "I mean a tremendously long beard. And I think it's a beard of all the sins of the people, and I think he sticks [the sins] in here. That's what makes his beard so long. He has a long beard, and long hair, and no nose [but has eyes]."

I asked her if God has ears.

"Of course he has ears," Stephanie replied, "or he couldn't hear our prayers! And he has this light that goes everywhere, like an aura . . . or a shaft of light."

Her image of God has no body, "because we're God's hands and feet."

Her picture of Jesus was not at all like her image of God. Jesus had a body and a hair of branches like a tree. She described the differences.

"See, Jesus," she explained, "instead of God with the long beard, Jesus has . . . this headpiece, and I'm all a piece of his head . . . this big crown he wears. And when I start to sin, the branches start to grow, and the more I sin, and then he reaches out to the branches.

And when I ask for forgiveness, and he knows that I'm sorry, that I would like him to forgive me, he takes it back. Sometimes, his crown is real full because people forget to say I'm sorry. But then sometimes, it come close to the root."

During this conversation, we talked about Jesus' relationship with Stephanie. It is Jesus who makes Stephanie sing, "because singing makes me happy, and Jesus wants to make me happy." I asked her how she makes Jesus happy. "By obeying God's word," she remarked. Then I asked her what word that was, and she answered by quoting from Matthew 11: "Come unto me. Good words to hear, when I think he's there." She admitted to feeling abandoned, left alone by Jesus sometimes. She yearns to hear the words "Come unto me." And that is where she places her life, in that place of great tension. She is caught between wanting to give all and come unto Jesus and resting in him, and trying to do it all on her own, which leaves her feeling abandoned. Stephanie does not know which way to go, and this leaves her feeling stuck.

These four moving stories fascinated me—these insightful stories of Christian faith told by young people who truly believe in the presence of God even though they are being treated in a secular institution. These stories are even more remarkable when one they are heard them behind the double-locked doors of a well-guarded "care" facility, where even staff members were forbidden to mention God or Jesus before my employment.[2]

In each of these four narratives, a child has come to a place where they have no independent power. All four of them have come to places in their Christian journeys where they are frozen and truly vulnerable to outside pressures. Physically and spiritually, they are in a state of bondage, held captive by parents, guardians, the state, or the institution. They are more than ready to hear about the good news of God's grace and to see it extended to them in the life of the church. Steve needs Christ's community to provide caring discipline and nurturing support, especially in light of his explosive relationship with his family. Randy's story needs to be embedded in the story-filled traditions and celebrations of the church. Randy loves stories and needs to be reminded of the other stories of God told by Christians and celebrated in our rituals. Dennis needs the community of believers to understand God is with him when he no longer understands God by himself. And Stephanie depends on the body of Christ to believe in Christ for her in her moments of doubt. All of these young people's important needs may best be met by the rich reservoir of resources found in Christ's body.

What has kept these children out of reach of Christ's community, from actual knowledge of God's grace, is complicated and painful. In some cases, the health-service system, embedded in the Enlightenment narrative about the power of "rational minds" and "self-righteous" theories of the social science, has fortified the barrier between church and state. As long as children are wards of the state, they are often removed from the church, and therefore from knowledge of God. Many publicly sponsored institutions of health care have recently diminished the role and function of churches and synagogues by phasing out chaplaincy programs. These institutions that seek to cure mind and body fail to acknowledge the necessity of caring for whole persons—mind, body, *and* spirit.

Sometimes the fault lies with the family, whether the family of origin or a therapeutic foster family. Given society's intolerance for differences among the human race—an intolerance manifest in many congregations and parishes—many parents and foster parents are afraid to bring children with disabilities to their home churches. They are scared or embarrassed of what other families will think about how the child looks, acts, or thinks. Wanting to spare the child and other family members the pain of being ostracized, they either hide the child or stop attending church.

Sometimes fault lies within the Christian community. Even though many mainline denominations have eloquent position papers stating why *all* people should be welcomed into the church, individual congregations and parishes sometimes act in a scandalous, inhospitable manner toward people with disabilities. For example, many children in that hospital came from families who had attended church regularly until a church leader told them that it would be best if they attended a different church. Many Christian communities believe they cannot adequately care for a family with a parent who has schizophrenia, a young boy with autistic behavior, or a young woman with Down's syndrome. The Christian community is often unaware that these families are unable to provide necessary day-to-day care without the prayerful, practical, caring love of Christ's people. If the family is doomed in our church, so is the child with a disability.

What the church fails to perceive is that each new person with a disability is a gift in the form of a stranger, a gift from God to the community. It is this stranger-as-gift who will teach the community how to care in a Christlike manner by making known to others the signs of God's grace in loving action. In the very act of trying to love others as God loved us, Christ's community is transformed by God's love. Acts of compassion that were once awkward become an integral part of the culture of a Christian community.

Why must the church welcome and take in *all* children, regardless of their abilities or limitations? Because Jesus said so. Jesus didn't tell us to do this because it would be easy (it won't be), or because it is what good societies ought to do (society isn't sure about what to do with these children). Jesus is telling the disciples of today—the church—to let the children come to the living body of Christ so that all may learn from them.

These young people are some of the "children" Jesus was talking about and wants us to bless, for they too will show us the proper stance toward receiving the reign of God. In the Gospel of Mark (10:13–16), Jesus becomes angry at the disciples for stopping parents from bringing their children forward to be touched and blessed. We are to be like children, confident that we are safe under God's protection and conscious of God's boundless love for us. In Jesus' day, children were considered their parents' property and therefore had no power of self-assertion. Jesus' disciples were to live a lifestyle of such self-denial, dependent on God's grace, eager to receive Christ's blessing as the proper stance before God in receiving the dominion of God.

In stories of children with disabilities, we learn from each child's powerlessness and dependence on Christ's community our own need for Christ today. Like Steve, we need the Christian community to train us in the ways of Christ. Just as Randy did, we need to hear, act out, and celebrate God's story throughout our lives. Like Dennis, we need a community of Christians who know God in order to know God ourselves. And like Stephanie, we need the community of Christian faith to help us in our times of doubt. By making their needs known to the church, these children teach other Christians what it is to be childlike in relationship with Christ, to be totally dependent upon the seemingly endless love of a caring other. These children are teaching the church, a gathering of human creatures, the proper position for living in this dependent relationship with God the Creator. *This* is the gestured posture Christians need to take in order to receive the dominion of God.

Perhaps Stephanie's situation best explains our current predicament. Stephanie told me that she longs to hear Jesus say, "Come to me all who are carrying heavy burdens . . . and I will give you rest" (Matt. 11). My hope is that Stephanie will someday hear these words when the church assumes its responsibility as Christ's body to let the children come to Christ. By welcoming these children into congregations and parishes, we welcome Christ into our hearts.

chapter nine

open house

The American Family
in the Household of God

When we hear the word *family*, what assumptions come to mind? To many, family means a modern nuclear family, usually biological, with one or two parents, two or so children, and perhaps a menagerie of pets. Family implies involvement in community activities such as school, ballet, soccer practice, and church. For others, family comes in different shapes and sizes. Scott Walker observes, "There aren't many maps for this new territory."[1] Social critic Stephanie Coontz has commented that the ideal of the American family (if there ever really was such a thing) is dissolving, if not actively participating in destroying itself before our very eyes. The patterns that define a family continue to change.[2]

One of the most powerful means of creating and reinforcing the stereotype of the nuclear family has been television. From *Ozzie and Harriet* in the 1950s to *Roseanne* in the 1990s, depictions of families on television have contributed to many people's perception of what family is. Such nuclear families, writes Stephanie Coontz, do have similar characteristics. To begin with, everything in these televized construction of families revolves around the mother, leaving father and mother in an awkward relationship. Most families who consider themselves "nuclear" are middle- to upper-middle-class white families, which are a creation of the European bourgeois culture of the nineteenth century. Civic holidays such as the Fourth of July are as important as religious holidays such as

Christmas and have become this country's new family holidays.[3]

Before the nineteenth century, the American family was quite different from today's icon of sweet wholesomeness. Family researcher Judith Stacey writes that, for the family in colonial America of the eighteenth century,

- All marriages were arranged.
- Boundaries between public and private lives were permeable, if present at all.
- Communities regulated proper family conduct to the point of actively intervening to enforce disciplinary codes of the township.
- Parents freely exchanged children as apprentices and servants with other families.[4]

(This model of colonial life is still evident in the ideals of Amish Christians. Among the Amish, spouses are chosen rationally, not romantically. Affection for one another comes *after* the wedding, not before, because of the danger of loving the spouse "inordinately.")

The Industrial Revolution destroyed this model of family life. During the Industrial Revolution, "family work" was considered to be qualitatively different from "productive work." Men started going out of the house to work rather than working at home. Love and companionship became the ideal purpose of marriage, and privacy assumed greater importance. And since men were no longer home, women became devoted to nurturing children. Motherhood was, and to many people still is, exalted as a natural and demanding vocation. "Super Mom" lives, for many families in America.

Theologian Rodney Clapp writes that, in the late twentieth century, many Christian families live by the following formula of family life:

Nuclear Family = Traditional Family = Natural Family = Biblical Family

But this equation is false. Clapp argues that there is no biblical mandate or support for the ideal American middle-class nuclear family. Sentimental, romantic notions of the family are alien to the biblical ideal of the family.[5]

Theologian Janet Fishburn understands how romantic idealization of the nuclear family threatens the community life of many churches. Fishburn rightly argues that we seek to worship the "Family Pew," the pew where the family would sit every Sunday, behind and in front of another family, and that attending church is where the American family shares their vision of good citizenship and family life. In this Family Pew, she suggests that we use religious language and religious rituals of the church to reinforce the nuclear family's commitments. What emerges is a superficial, controlling folk religion, in which believers use God as a means to achieve their ends—the support of their family in the cast of nineteenth-century bourgeois values.[6] The lines between God, family, church, and nationalism are soon blurred, and these bits and pieces are rearranged to suit the needs of the family. Soon, rather than family members serving God in the context of a church, God serves the needs of the family in the home, with no need for church. The family is now the central context for worshiping God.

This worship of family as an idol raises a central question: What is the appropriate role and function of the family in the context of the church? Rodney Clapp states it well in his preacher-like admonition: the truth is that the family is *not* God's most important institution on earth. The family is *not* the social agent that makes, and most significantly shapes and forms, the character of Christians. The family is *not* the primary vehicle of God's grace and salvation for a world on the edge of despair.[7]

Instead, it is the *church* that is God's most important gathering on earth. The church is the the primary vehicle for the good news of God's gift of grace and salvation, given startling clarity by the life, death, and resurrection of Jesus Christ. Jesus called his disciples and followers to be part not of the *family* of God, but of the *household* of God.

By contemporary standards, a household of biblical Israel would be considered a commune. The average Jewish household comprised from fifty to a hundred people. Our ideal nuclear family would be a small part of a larger household, and three such large families were usually united by arranged marriage to form clans (Josh. 7:17).[8]

What Jesus' ministry did was nothing less than reconfigure how we are to understand ourselves and our biological kin. In Mark 3:31–35, Jesus says that his *primary* family is not composed of genetic ancestors only, but also includes those who share his obedient spirit. Jesus was not denying the importance of his biological family. Instead, Jesus was broadening our perception of family into the inclusive context of the household of God. Jesus greatly expanded our lineage, calling us to new relationships, with responsibilities and accountability to one another:

> Do not think that I have come to bring peace to the earth. . . . For I have come to set a man against his father, and a daughter against her mother. . . . Whoever loves father or mother more than me is not worthy of me; and whoever loves son or daughter more than me is not worthy of me." (Matt. 10:34–39)

Of course, Jesus did not intend to entirely diminish the importance of the biological family. He reaffirms what the family does toward spreading the news of the coming of the dominion of God, fulfilling what had begun at the beginning of creation. Consider Matthew 19:3–12, where Jesus places marriage in the goodness of creation, instructing this followers that "what God has joined together, let no one put asunder." Jesus surprised even his own disciples by calling children to come to him for a blessing. By Jesus' ministry, we come to understand that the family, with its own standards and values free from the practices of a worshiping community, is not the vehicle of salvation. For those who follow Jesus, the critical bloodline that guides and nurtures our character is not biological, but rather divine.

What good does this knowledge of how Jesus understood families as part of the household of God do for us today? It provides Christians with a map for locating our primary family among society's attempts to redefine family. Because of the wisdom of the gospel story, practiced in our Christian traditions, we need not be caught up in the struggle to find a new definition.

For many families who have suffered great traumas, the message that each family unit is not meant to do everything in life by itself may be just what they need to hear. In my experience, the families who have suffered the most at the hands of society are families who have children with disabilities. Many families with such children have been left to traverse thickly overgrown paths in unknown territory in order to seek out care for their children.

Consider the story of Mary and Michael,[9] the proud parents of two beautiful children, a college-aged daughter and a son, Philip. An exceptional athlete, Philip has Down's syndrome, but it has not kept him from being engaged in life. Mary and Michael and their children are an affluent, upper-middle-class family who attend a large mainline Protestant church. While they would be considered "model Christians" by most pastors, they have raised disturbing questions about how the church has acted toward Philip. Mary feels the church has dealt, at best, awkwardly with her son. She is always having to advise the church how to engage her son in the normal church activities, including worship, Sunday school, and youth groups. She has at times been enraged by a church that doesn't know how to support her family.

Tired of constantly asking and telling the church what to do, Mary took the counsel of a close friend, who also has a child with a disability. The friend told Mary to separate God from the church and not expect anything of the church. All her expectations should be placed on God, *outside* the context of the church. Since she has adopted this perspective, Mary says, she feels much better.

What Mary did was the same thing many families do as they encounter obstacles in finding services for their children with disabilities. By enduring the setbacks and celebrating the triumphs in Philip's life separately and not in community, though, Philip's family and the church are failing to live up to the sacrament of Philip's baptism. In baptism, a child is recognized as a gift not only to the biological family, but also as a precious gift to the congregation in the household of God.[10] Through baptism, the church announces to the world that it is an "open house" for those called to be part of the body of Christ—regardless of their abilities or disabilities.

Life with a child with a disability is unpredictable—as is life with any child. Churches benefit greatly from guiding and nurturing these children, realizing in the process that there are even more ways than imaginable to be in the body of Christ. Children with disabilities often embody the gift of evangelism, creating a caring community around them. These children encourage congregations to find alternative ways of expressing the gospel, ways that would never have been developed if that particular child had not been in their midst.

There are some who will learn in the presence of these children the art of celebrating the simple joys of life—the sight of a smiling child with a disability saying "ice cream" in sign language, for example. And some will learn the importance of solidarity with a child when health-care opportunities are being eliminated.

All of this is possible because, by the gift of Jesus Christ, we realize that we are not isolated, nuclear families. Rather, we have been welcomed into Christ's open house, sisters and brothers in the household of God.

chapter ten

formation and transformation at camp ahus

We arrived at Camp Ahus outside Kristianstad in southern Sweden at seven-thirty in the morning after a night train trip from Stockholm. Throughout our time in Stockholm and Uppsala, our host had talked about this "most special confirmation camp" for young people with disabilities as well as those with none. I assumed that this summer camp would be like those I had visited in the States, where a handful of people with disabilities are guided, cared for, and strongly protected by a larger group of well-intentioned young people. Instead, I found a confirmation camp that changed my image of summer youth activities.

Thirty-two young people—sixteen with disabilities and sixteen without—live together from mid-June to mid-July, sharing in all their daily activities. The disabilities included mental retardation, autism, emotional disturbances, and physical and learning difficulties. If it weren't for certain physical features of some of the disabilities, however, it would have been difficult to tell who among the young people had a disabling condition and who did not.

Sponsored by the Church of Sweden, Ahus (pronounced Oh-hoos), or Camp Arrow, is located on a wooded parcel of land shared by another branch of the Church of Sweden and a scout troop. The summer program is a very popular way for Swedish youth to be confirmed in the church.

The cabin's inhabitants were just starting to stir as we drove down the dirt road toward the wooden chapel. Morning showers were running full blast, and young people were poking their heads out of cabin windows, trying to catch a glimpse of the American tourists. The campers had spent much of the previous day teaching each other English greetings, so we were warmly welcomed at breakfast with loud cries of "Good morning!" and "How is it with you?" One young woman with Down's syndrome gave me the thumbs-up sign and would say "Sure thing!" whenever I said anything in my fractured Swedish-English.

Not only had the youths worked together in learning some English, but they were responsible for informing each other about the daily news of the camp, the nation, and the world. After breakfast, one disabled teenager teamed up with someone without a disability and dramatically told of the day's news, using the camp activities list and the local newspaper as a script. The group moaned at the announcement that Sweden had lost the World Soccer Cup, they shouted "hooray" for the visiting Americans, and they spoke in hushed tones about increased U.S. aid to the Nicaraguan contras. After the news, the entire group stood together in a circle, holding hands while praying. Then they all ran out of the dining hall, eager to begin the day's activities.

Youth who were disabled paired off with those who were not disabled, forming a "buddy system" for the duration of the camp month. In choosing to share their lives with one another, the youth also accepted the responsibility of forming and informing one another in the daily tasks of life. Thus they did *everything* together— from playing soccer to learning Scripture verses. One boy told me that the theme of the camp was two-ness. "We do everything together," he said. "We always think of two, not one, person."

These young people were intimately involved in the ongoing process of forming one another and learning about the Christian faith and the church of Sweden. Their images of each other are also being transformed in this context. The camp was originally envisioned as a place where teens would be free and secure enough to become acquainted with their individual limitations, regardless of either their disabilities or their gifts. The camp's directors and its pastor told me that, although the young people learn to touch their weaknesses in life, they also come to realize that Jesus Christ's active presence in their community is what enables them to recognize and celebrate each person's different gifts and talents.

The pastor emphasized that the young people with disabilities have as much to teach us about the learning to live with limitations as they need to learn about accepting someone else's abilities. "These handicapped youth stare us in the face and encourage and empower us to stare in the face of God who is in their lives," he explained. "They are our teachers as they allow us to live with them, stand with them, work with them, and be with them. We cannot force ourselves on them; we need to respect them, and they already respect us. In turn, they look us in the face and give us the courage to find out how to live with them. This allows us to simply be with them in life and community. That is all they ask. That is all that God asks."

It was exciting to watch this transformation take place in the relationships among the campers. Given the opportunity to query the young people about life at Camp Ahus, I first asked the non-disabled campers what it was like to be with youth who were disabled. The teenagers responded by saying that they were learning "gentleness and love" and "a new way of being a friend." Some said that it was stressful to live with those who were disabled because you "just can't do everything together." But someone else quickly added that they were learning patience, learning to move more slowly to accommodate the other person.

One youth remarked that it was a "different world here; one dares to be oneself, out of pure joy, and to give and receive hugs." He also said that, at other times, they were "learning to become angry, and not be scared of that anger, but to deal directly with one another." Those who were not disabled were learning how those who are disabled feel: "No one is perfect—we are always growing. This is the theme of Ahus, is it not?"

The youth with disabilities were also experiencing changes in their image of themselves and others. Coming from a world in which their disabilities and limitations had always been the focus of attention, they were learning how to accept their abilities and gifts in a community of successful, healthy peers. To be sure, some felt "stressed out" by those of companions who sometimes moved too fast. But the majority were enjoying this "good time."

One young man, who had tried the preceding school year to make it in a "normal" school but had eventually been placed in a "special" school, said: "At the old school, it is too tough, not easy. I am mad at school, frustrated and angry at all times. Now, at camp, I feel like this is the way it should be, living with each other." And a young woman with Down's syndrome told me that she liked it here at Ahus. "Freedom is coming. Yes, I know, for sure!" she exclaimed with her customary thumbs-up sign and infectious smile.

The most memorable experience of community during my visit was in the evening soccer game between Camp Ahus and a neighboring Church of Sweden confirmation camp that does not enroll people with disabilities. Emphasizing that the goal of the game was fun, not winning, the Camp Ahus team—with a raucous cheering section shouting "Give me an A-M-E-N . . . what does it spell?" marched onto the field.

The game was a model of integration. Everyone had a chance to play. The goalie, a young boy with a learning disability, seemed anything but disabled when it came to catching some very fast soccer balls aimed at the Ahus net. While the other team usually had one fast player on the ball, the Ahus team clumped together in packs of three or four to negotiate the ball down the field.

Most important, the Ahus team had fun. They laughed whenever the ball came their way, and they shouted cheers like "Give me some G-R-A-C-E . . . GRACE!" They hugged one another whenever the ball came close to a net or made a goal. The score couldn't have been better—a four-to-four tie, with everyone a winner.

What I saw at Camp Ahus was a story of formation and transformation taking place in a community of Christian faith. All the young people were in the process of forming and educating one another while sharing common tasks in being a camp community together. But they were also involved in transformation, encouraging one another to respect themselves and others out of their love for Jesus Christ and the world God created.

The transformation occurred as teenagers with disabilities began to understand their gifts and abilities. And those with seemingly no disabilities learned to accept life's limitations. "I have learned to treat differently the handicapped person on the street," one youth said. "The memory of the camp is always in us, in our hearts."

chapter eleven

the place and power of acceptance in pastoral care with persons who are mentally retarded

In pastoral counseling, acceptance has often been understood as the counselor's ability to help a client discover a place to feel less threatened.[1] But when acceptance involves acknowledging a person's condition as "mentally retarded," the issue becomes more complex and emotionally charged. For persons who are mentally retarded, acceptance—by both self and others—involves exploring one's identity in relationship with others, leading to a broader knowledge about oneself. However, these people are stuck with a label that often conceals their potential gift. A disability like mental retardation influences not only how they view themselves, but also how their families, pastors, and Christian community accept them.

I begin with the story of John, someone who rejected the label of "mental retardation" and learned who he truly is. When I met him, John was in his mid-twenties, living in an institution for people who are mentally retarded. He has cerebral palsy, which limits the use of his legs and affects his speech. He also has dyslexia, a learning disability that prevents him from being able to read. Through accepting some of the limitations of his disabilities, John has learned to explore the broader use of his abilities and gifts. Although he cannot read or write, John can talk, and he listens to other people extremely well. He also has an excellent memory. In other words, he has all the gifts of a born storyteller.

In a conversation we had about acceptance, John stated clearly that he had always felt accepted by God: "Or else God wouldn't have made me or put me here on earth," he told me. But John had not felt loved or accepted by his biological family early in life. Before John's birth, John's mother and father had been living on welfare and working odd jobs whenever possible. When John was born, his father took off and was never seen again. John's mother, alone and overwhelmed by the burden of caring for another child in addition to the four girls she already had, gave John up for adoption at age three. For years, John believed that she'd given him up because of his disability, and he felt rejected. Not until he was nine did John learn the truth: his mother could not afford to pay for the corrective surgery and physical therapy John needed.

John lived in three different foster homes. He told me he couldn't remember the first home, but the second one he recalled as the "most abusive": "They never hugged me. They put me on a chair and tied me down so I wouldn't fall off, or kept me in bed until sores would start to appear." At other times, John was expected to crawl to the bathroom when he needed to, without the use of a wheelchair. If he didn't make it in time, one of his foster parents would put him in a cold bath for more than an hour to clean him off, hoping this would "encourage" him to do better the next time. The third foster family took much better care of John. They were affectionate and took care of his medical bills. They even tried to help him walk. But the parents in this home were in ill health, and John had to leave. He was then placed in an institution for the mentally retarded. He was six years old.

Even though John doesn't appear to be mentally retarded, he believes the institution gave him the label because of his reading disability. In retrospect, John thinks it was a good placement, though, because he got the physical therapy he needed, and he feels they taught him as well as anyone could. It was there that John learned to be more independent, to move his wheelchair around the campus, which gave him some degree of autonomy.

John has had varied experiences with faith communities. He has attended both denominational and nondenominational Christian churches. He remembers first taking God seriously at age thirteen.

He sees as evidence that God loves him the fact that, with all his moves to different foster homes and institutions, he did not die. His most painful experience involved the pastor of a small church who was sure that John's disability was caused by the devil. When this pastor tried to "exorcise" the devil, John was sure they were going to kill him.

John's acceptance of himself has resulted from his recent experience of being accepted and loved for who he is within a local congregation. A small group from the church has come to talk with him "as if I really had a brain!" He says that others who had come in the past had "talk[ed] to us adults as if we were really little kids; drives me crazy." Feeling accepted by a congregation for who he is gives John the freedom to explore other options for his future in the larger community outside the institution.

John has moved from a poor self-image, stemming from a lack of acceptance by the people around him, to self-acceptance and an appreciation of what his disability has actually enabled him to accomplish in his short life within the context of a Christian community. When I asked what would happen if his disabilities were taken away, John said he'd lose his large arm muscles because he would not be using his arms to move his wheelchair anymore.

> Let's put it this way: Your ability, if you are close to God, comes with spirit. If you take away your ability, your spirit dies. If you take away my disability, I probably couldn't tell stories; but it's all teamwork, between God and myself. I've looked back on this disability. I probably would've been wilder without the disability. But the disability gives me strength. I ask God to continue to give me the energy to get around. And I do that pretty well with the wheelchair. The disability used to get me down because I used to be so slow. But people who think I can't do anything from this are always surprised when God and I get together. It's okay for you to prevent my getting hurt, but don't prevent God and John from doing things together.

John understands God's acceptance of him as grace, and he knows that God is patient with him, allowing him to go slow when he needs to and accepting him when "I'm so damned stupid, as we all are." John believes that he is held fast by the love of God in this world.

A Higher Barrier to Acceptance

Often people approach a person with disabilities such as John intellectually, knowing that the person is a human being endowed with some abilities but is hampered in some respects by a disabling condition. The non-disabled person tries to imagine what it would be like to live without the full use of his or her own legs or cognitive abilities. Many then find themselves suffering *for* the person who is disabled. Unable to focus on the person, they focus on the disability. This confusion of focus makes it difficult to be with a person who is disabled. Human dialogue is abruptly cut off and a perceptual and attitudinal barrier is put in place.

A disabling condition such as mental retardation can sometimes become a symbol that shapes how individuals with that disability envision themselves and how other people—the person's family, pastor, and Christian community—imagine the person. This can happen in several ways. First, although some professionals argue that labels can serve as passports to improved educational services for persons with disabilities, many people are more scared of their "disabled" labels than they are of their disabling conditions.[2] One young woman with a physical disability said that, although a disability can interfere with the practical running of one's life, it is the reaction and non-action of society that causes the most problems for persons with disabilities:

> The "sick role" is society's niche for THE DISABLED. You must behave as "the sick" at all times but never complain about it. You must allow your person to have good works vented upon it, it makes THEM feel better, accept with a gracious smile offers of "help" you don't need.[3]

Second, the individual who is disabled is surrounded by a family who struggles with the stigma of the "handicapped" label. Many times, the birth of a child with mental retardation is not treated as a happy event but as a crisis. Some see it as a symbol of divine retribution for some forgotten sin of the parents. Unlike the bouncing, happy babies on the covers of magazines in hospital waiting rooms, the child born with a disability may be lethargic, unable to respond to her mother's touch, and hooked to machines and monitors that are necessary to detail any changes in growth. Family therapists write that the first emotional reaction of new parents in seeing their child with a disabling condition is one of shock and denial at the loss of what was to be a "normal, happy baby."[4]

Third, many times clergy exhibit great sensitivity to the immediate needs of the family in the crisis-like atmosphere surrounding the birth of a child with a disability. There is a great need among pastors, however, to understand the complex concerns and ethical dilemmas that surround such a child and influence the family's reaction to the child's presence in their life. If a pastor envisions the child with a disability as a symbol of suffering, the primary focus may again be on the disability rather than on the child's needs or the family's capacity to adapt to the child's condition. Some pastors who have entered into the challenge of accepting a person with a disability admit that what they see in that person is their own finitude, helplessness, and powerlessness.

Paul Tillich has written that, although the problems of life may appear "too profound" for anyone, the real truth is that nothing is too profound for God. It is because we become too uncomfortable that we shy away from the truth.[5] A theological framework that emphasizes the *child* with a disability as one who is created in God's image needs to be explored and articulated. Helmut Thielicke, for example, has called persons with severe disabilities "off-duty image[s] of God."[6] From a theological standpoint, accepting people with disabilities is of primary importance in helping those people accept themselves as valuable members of a Christian community, as human beings who have also been created in the image of God. The goal of family members, the pastor, the person who is disabled, and the congregation is not denial of the condition, but engagement of other characteristics of this individual who has much to give within the body of Christ.

A Theological Reflection on Acceptance

The theological context for accepting a person who is mentally re-tarded begins with the premise that all human beings have been created in God's image. Because we are created in God's image, we are born and nurtured in a relational bond with God, a bond that is reified in the Christian community. We perceive and understand this relationship in a unique fashion, as each of us is a new creation. It is within the church that we are given the opportunity to explore and discover what gifts and talents we bring into the body of Christ, and this theological task can be broken down into four parts.

First, we must acknowledge that all human beings are created in the image of God. This simple yet profound belief is repeated in the creation stories recorded in Genesis. It is vital to remember that human beings did not make themselves or any other part of creation. Although this truth may appear obvious, the essential humanness of the person who is mentally retarded remains a point of contention within our society. According to the ethicist Joseph Fletcher, the two primary criteria for determining the humanness of persons who are mentally retarded should be intellectual ability and relational ability. Fletcher states, "Any individual of the species homo sapiens who falls below the I.Q. 20 mark in a standard Stanford-Binet test is not a person."[7] The Anglican Church of Canada used human relationships as a requirement for personhood when it advocated euthanasia, arguing that "the creature looks like a human being and that it was born of woman, though we know that it cannot possibly develop 'humanhood.'"[8]

Second, we must recognize that God has given us the ability to have relationships with God and other human beings. It is this very relationship between God and humanity that influences and shapes human nature. Being human has been defined as the extent to which we can reach out and provide care for those who cry for love.[9] But it is also the ability to cry for love, to admit that we are truly in need of being with others. To be human is both to admit one's need for love and to be able to love others.

Communication between persons who are and are not disabled has been a major barrier to participation in congregational life for those with disabilities. Like John, many people are labeled "mentally retarded" because of an inability to express their thoughts or feelings in speech or writing. And some who are mentally retarded may perceive and understand the world in other, more sensorial ways—through movements, colors, and sounds. It is these people whose "humanity" is questioned by professionals. Research on alternative forms of communication, such as American Sign Language (ASL), is constantly being debated by professionals who explore alternative symbol systems that may provide avenues through which persons who are mentally retarded might "prove their humanity" by communicating with others.

The third part of this theological task is recognizing that we are given the gift of creativity *within* certain boundaries. Biblical scholar Walter Brueggemann correctly understands that our destiny is to live in God's world, with God's creation, on God's terms, as God's people.[10] Each of God's people contributes something new and incommunicably tender to the life of the earth.[11] Each person who is considered "mentally retarded" by society has been endowed by God with unique gifts and creative talents that are to be shared within the household of God.

It is important not to overromanticize a person's disabling condition, but it is equally important to understand that there are many ways to relate to God and to others in this world. If John, the young man with cerebral palsy, could read and write, we might have lost a great storyteller. If he were not in a wheelchair, as he himself said, he would have had little reason to build up such strong arm muscles. If we take away the disabling condition, we may run the risk of taking away the person.

The fourth part of this task is to recognize that the gifts of each person in the faith community are essential to the life of the community. The apostle Paul reminded the early Christian church, which was wondering what gifts and talents were most important, that in a unified yet diverse body of Christ, each member has a gift from God that is to be used in serving the church. The whole church could not remain alive without each person being active in the church's life, no matter how an individual's ability was perceived within the community. For Paul, each person brought an invaluable contribution to the body of Christ.[12] Each person is loved by God, and is an important member of the church.

Another way to understand such acceptance is as gift of grace and faith. Theologian Douglas John Hall writes that faith in such grace confesses that "God is willing to use the raw stuff of our deeds and misdeeds in the same manner as God used primeval chaos to create a world."[13] In Christian community we remember and retell how God uses God's people—deeds and misdeeds, able-bodied and disabled alike—to give birth to wonder.

Baptism: To Live Out Acceptance in the Church

This theological rationale in a Christian community is often first recognized in the sacramental ritual of baptism. In the Christian church, the sacrament of baptism calls God's people together to accept all people into the life of this story-formed gathering. Within the church, pastoral care for those with mental retardation may begin with their baptism. Baptism is an essential step in helping the community at large to appreciate and accept the person as an invaluable part of the body of Christ. It is a sign and seal of God's loving initiative in first creating humankind and of our incorporation into the body of Christ.[14]

It is an amazing phenomenon within the Christian church that not everyone who wants to be baptized is allowed to be. Many parents tell stories of having their requests to have infants with mental retardation baptized denied by a pastor or church's ruling body. Sometimes the request is denied because the child causes personal discomfort for the pastor; sometimes the church doubts that a child would understand the sacrament. John's story earlier in this chapter illustrates the importance of baptism: it was the first time John felt accepted by someone else. John believes we should be baptized

> because Jesus did it. But you do it for more than that. You do it to show that you're washing away the old self: when you go down, you're buried with Christ; when you arise out of the water, you rise with Christ. You're part of a new covenant. You do it with community who embraces you.

In the World Council of Churches' manual, *Baptism, Eucharist, and Ministry*, baptism is said to have two important purposes. First, it is a sign of new life through Jesus Christ.[15] It means participating in the life, death, and resurrection of Jesus, who was baptized in the Jordan River. Once baptized, we will be ultimately one with Christ as we are further nurtured and guided by the Holy Spirit within the church.

Second, one is baptized into the body of Christ.[16] Through baptism, the congregation acknowledges that we are members of one another.[17] An important implication of baptism for the person who is mentally retarded—as well as for that person's family and pastor—is not only the recognition as a member of this community, but the community's reaffirmation of its own faith in God. The community pledges to provide an environment of witness and service to the life of the newly baptized.[18]

Baptism is a powerful, tangible ritual that is bound to have an impact on a person with mental retardation for a number of reasons. First, baptism is important as a symbolic act, with its sprinkling or immersion in water "washing away our sins." Even people who are severely or profoundly mentally retarded react to the sensation of water on their bodies—with a scream, perhaps, or a giggle of delight. That they are responding is important, for it means that the event may be one they remember.

Second, for the family and the larger congregation, this symbolic act is an important first step in accepting the person with a disability as part of God's unfolding story of creation. The family and the congregation pledge to provide an environment of witness and service to the baptized person. This includes nurturing on a one-to-one level, as well as pursuing ways the person may participate in the life of the community. The congregation recognizes that the person has a place in the community when he or she is at worship, where the congregation re-creates the possibility of openness to God.[19]

Finally, the pastor is acting out the denomination's theological convictions regarding the place of persons with disabilities in the Christian community. The pastor puts the denomination's theological stance into human action in the context of the liturgy. By baptizing a person with mental retardation, the pastor is affirming that the person needs to be encouraged by other members of Christ's body, united in a single purpose, to become who God has created this person to be.[20]

At the beginning of this chapter, we read John's story, a story of acceptance in which we see God's grace in action. John believes that acceptance begins when you realize that God has a hold on you, and that you just have to hold on to God. If one understands this connection, it is easier to accept oneself in the community of Christian love. For John, acceptance means new hope for the future—"knowing that you are loved, and that God is going to work with you right where you are in this life."

People with mental retardation and other disabilities have much to teach us about acceptance—and about hope. My own hope for the future is that pastors, Christian educators, lay leaders, pastoral counselors, and congregations will work toward helping others accept the truth that people who are disabled are already accepted and loved by an ever-gracious God.

chapter twelve

letters to a
disabled church

Dear Pastor Smith:[1]

This is a hard letter for me to write, so please forgive any awkward-
ness in what is to follow. Let me begin by thanking you and this
church for welcoming our family. Since we moved from Oregon to
Ohio a year ago, we have been searching for a church that would
welcome and involve all the members of our family, both in worship and in the daily life of the congregation. My wife and I are
enjoying singing in the choir, as well as listening to your challenging sermons and meeting with others to read Scripture. Our ten-
year-old son is growing in his understanding of the Christian faith
in mission opportunities in the neighborhood.

However, I am writing this letter about our eight-year-old daughter, Carolyn, who attends the church's third-grade Sunday school
class. As you know, Carolyn's behavioral problems were so severe
last Sunday (she had an uncontrollable tantrum) that she had to be
taken out of the class by two adults. I also understand that the
teacher, Sally, does not want Carolyn back in the class, which is
why I'm writing you this letter.

As my wife and I have told you and the church's session, Carolyn
was recently tested at the University and diagnosed as borderline
mentally retarded with behavioral problems. She is also prone to

seizures, for which she receives medication. She is in the third grade in public school, and she seems to work well in that context with the help of an aide. She has never had a tantrum at school, so I was quite surprised to learn of the tantrum problems in Sunday school.

I am aware that there have been other problems with Carolyn in this class. When Carolyn first started the class, Sally invited me to visit the class any time I wanted. On the Sunday morning in September when I accompanied Carolyn to Sunday school, I was surprised to find that Sally was not in in the classroom at nine o'clock. Fifteen third-grade children were milling about in the room with no adult supervision. There was no one to welcome the children, no music playing, no one bringing the children together for an activity. Minute by minute, the children in the room grew louder and more active, Carolyn included. Because I was concerned, I stayed in the room until Sally arrived five minutes late. I later learned that this tardiness is routine, and that the children are routinely left unsupervised.

In the beginning, Sally told me that Carolyn was a joy to have in class. I have since learned through the church grapevine that there were situations where Carolyn had torn other children's artwork, refused to participate in games, and talked out loud during the retelling of the Bible story. When I learned of these incidents, I asked Sally why she hadn't told me about them. In reply, Sally asked me not to bring Carolyn to class this coming Sunday; she didn't think she could have Carolyn in the class anymore.

What is most dismaying about this situation is that I have taught the Sunday school teachers and youth group leaders how to work with children with disabilities. In the church where we were members in Oregon, I watched young people who had worked with Carolyn go on to study special education in college because they enjoyed being around children like Carolyn. I am always amazed how God uses Carolyn to inspire others into Christian ministry that includes those who are disabled.

My wife and I are very sorry about this situation. Is there anything we can do to make it possible for Carolyn—and therefore us—to stay in this church? If Carolyn cannot be welcomed as a baptized child of God in the life of this church because of her disability, does that also mean we will not be welcomed when we are older and also having a hard day in the body of Christ?

Sincerely yours,
Harold Bell

• • •

November 13, 1993

Dear Mr. Bell,

On behalf of this church family, let me say how grateful I am for your good letter. We are so blessed by your family's participation in the life of this church, and I would not desire to see anything deter your participation here.

Thank you for addressing the concern regarding your daughter's situation. I am sorry that it has taken me so long to get back to you. We discussed your situation among the elders of the church last night and have also discussed it with the Director of Christian Education and her staff, including Sally. In hindsight, we probably should have invited you and your wife to this meeting. I first thought that we would have some message of hope, some positive solution, to Carolyn's situation, but I'm afraid we've come up against some real obstacles that will need your attention.

You must understand that Carolyn is a difficult child for any Sunday school class, let alone for the church as a whole. We don't want to seem uncaring and insensitive to the special needs that children like Carolyn have in Sunday school classes. Please don't misunderstand: We want Carolyn in our church, as well as the rest of your family. We have tried to put ourselves in your position, to "walk a mile in your moccasins," carrying the exceptional burden that Carolyn presents to your family. We do this because we want you and your family to find the joy of living in Jesus in this church.

However, things have changed in this church, and we may not be doing well in serving Carolyn's extraordinarily demanding needs. We don't think you are fully aware of the kinds of problems we've had with Carolyn in Sunday school. Many Sundays, more than one adult has been required in Carolyn's Sunday school class, just because of Carolyn. On occasion, I have even had to go to the classroom to help deal with Carolyn. If Carolyn is bored and wants attention, she starts throwing Bibles and pulling other children's hair. Attendance has increased in all of the Sunday school classes except the class with Carolyn in it. There are students and parents who avoid Sunday school, solely because of Carolyn. This is not helpful for Carolyn or the other students, and we need to be sensitive to the other students and their families.

Our problem is this. We are not like the public schools, where a teacher and an aide who have an ongoing relationship with Carolyn are able to navigate the changes in her behavior. In Sunday school, teachers and children are constantly changing, and there is little if any consistency in the lesson material, let alone the way it is taught. Therefore, it would be better for all concerned if Carolyn no longer came to Sunday school.

If you have any questions about this letter, please feel free to contact me. We would be happy to talk with you at any time. And we will help you find a new church home. I wish I could be more hopeful, but I'm sure you understand our situation.

> In Christ's love,
> Pastor Smith

· · ·

April 6, 1994

Dear Rev. Hal:

Thank you for your visit to our home this past month. We are grateful that you showed such interest in our family and in Carolyn's participation in worship. We have looked high and low for a church such as First Church and hope to have finally found a church where we can all worship God. We hope to be able to call First Church home. I hope that even my son, who has decided not to attend any church (due to the experiences with our previous congregation), will want to be involved again in the life of the church.

Since our discussion of the problems Carolyn was having in Sunday school, we wanted to touch base and make sure she was doing better. My wife and I understand that the college student who is majoring in special education is working out well as an aide. We realize that the third-grade class is one of the largest in the church, and we thank you and the Sunday school staff for taking Carolyn into the class. Please let us know if there an aide will be needed for Vacation Bible School this summer, and we'll get working on finding someone.

I also thank you for letting me come to the church's session meeting, as well as the Christian Education committee meeting. It is often hard for people to understand the unique abilities, gifts, and opportunities Carolyn brings into the life of a church until someone points it out to them. Teaching people the practice of seeing and appreciating the intricacies of Carolyn's gifts to the church is similar to teaching people the practice of looking and comprehending the many messages going on simultaneously in a complex work of art. Who knows? You may even find more families with children with disabilities coming to your church because of the way you have availed yourself, and the church has opened itself up, to us and our family.

Thank you for opening the doors of welcome not only to our daughter, but also to our family as a whole. We have sensed the warmth of Christ-like hope in your gestures of welcome.

Many thanks,
Harold Bell

• • •

October 23, 1994
Dear Mr. Bell:

Let me begin by thanking you for keeping me and the session of this church informed of all the educational opportunities available regarding churches and handicapped children. You are a tireless advocate not only for Carolyn, but for other families with children like Carolyn. I also thank you, although belatedly, for telling other families with handicapped children about your experiences at this church, which is why this letter is so difficult to write.

I want to say how very sorry I am that you feel that Carolyn, you, and your family are not welcomed here anymore. There is, however, a problem with Carolyn's coming to Sunday school. First, it is questionable whether this would be the best environment for Carolyn, as there are so many children her age but without her handicap in the class. You must consider how this will affect the other children in the class. Besides, parents are starting to take their children out of this particular Sunday school class.

Second, the real problem is that there is no one to work and worship with Carolyn; we have no money to hire anyone to be with your daughter during Sunday school. I'm sure you wouldn't want Carolyn to just sit there without receiving any kind of religious instruction. If you or your wife would like to come with Carolyn and work with us in providing Christian instruction to her, that would be marvelous. However, if you are unable or unwilling to provide that, why then do you lay the burden at our feet? Carolyn is your family's responsibility, not ours.

We would desire efficient, effective ministry to Carolyn, but we are limited in our ability to do just that for Carolyn, due to her handicap. Remember: effective ministry must involve a cooperative effort! In other cases, the parents and the paid volunteer must be there for this highly specialized ministry. Carolyn's condition is such that she requires a well-trained, paid assistant. If you can provide that, then let's talk about how to coordinate such an arrangement.

If you cannot provide this assistance, then I will do all I can to help find you and your family a new church home. Know that my prayers will be with you, your family, and Carolyn. I know that God has a special congregation in mind for you, and I pray that you will find it soon.

With God's blessings,
Rev. Hal

• • •

March 14, 1995

Dear Pastor Anne:

On behalf of this family, I write to you as one who is tired. As a family, we are tired of "church shopping," a ritual we Protestants perform whenever we move to a new area. We have been to so many churches in the year and a half since we moved here from Oregon that my wife no longer volunteers to sing in choir, afraid we will need to move once again because of Carolyn's situation. I confess that I secretly long for a more authoritative polity, one that would tell congregations and families that we stay together and work things out. Who knows? Perhaps we would all turn to the Holy Spirit, who would then be impelled to grace us with imagination in our struggle to be the body of Christ. Is this a foolish desire?

The note you sent home on Sunday regarding your "concern" that Carolyn is not fitting in in her Sunday school classroom because "she is too much a bother" is troubling. Carolyn has been excited about the class and enjoys spending time with her friends there, because many of them are the same children she goes to school with during the week. It seemed to us to be a better situation than any we have found in the three other churches we've tried to join since moving here. We understand that Carolyn's needs present many unique challenges, but we had hoped that, because of Carolyn's friendship with the other children and their friendship with her, things would work out well this time.

Please understand that we are willing to help train a volunteer or help pay for someone to serve as an aide during Sunday school class. Please let us know what we need to do in order to ensure that Carolyn will continue to be part of Sunday school. We are very tired, and we long to find our place in and among a community of Christians.

>   With hope,
>   Harold Bell

• • •

April 2, 1995

Dear Mr. Bell:

Your letter of March 14 makes this letter difficult to write. I know that you and your family yearn to be find a home in a congregation, and I so wished that this could have been the case with this church.

Unfortunately, in talking with the Sunday school teacher about Carolyn's participation in the classroom, we do not believe we have the volunteer or paid staff necessary to meet Carolyn's handicapped needs. Because of this, I am not confident that this setting would be a positive experience for Carolyn. I *am* confident that it is *not* a positive experience for the Sunday school teacher and her class when Carolyn is in class. This doesn't mean that Carolyn doesn't need religious instruction and Christian fellowship, but I am sorry to say I do not believe our current program or church offers anything that can meet Carolyn's handicapped needs.

In rereading the letter you gave me from Pastor Smith (September 1, 1993), I think that his church would be the best place for you to attend. They are smaller in size, and you have theological connections there since you were brought up in this mainline Protestant denomination, which is an asset.

Be assured that we are not excluding or prohibiting Carolyn from this church; all I am saying is I do not believe my church can be of any help to Carolyn or your family. I am sorry that we are not presently able to do more.

> With Christ's love,
> Pastor Anne

Part three

❧

The Church as Servant

chapter thirteen

to play
is to care

A primary theme in a hospital setting, whether the hospital treats acute care patients or children with disabilities, is care. Pastoral counselors, nurses, doctors, social workers, special educators, secretaries, and housekeepers in hospitals are invested in doing one essential task for the patient and for one another—*care*.

The importance of care is captured in two memories from my work with children who have emotional and behavioral disabilities. The first dramatizes the supreme value of care, which was obviously missing from the life of Jerry,[1] a young man of fifteen with an emotional disability. On the day that is etched in my memory, things had not gone well for Jerry, and he was angry. In an eloquent, two-minute speech before the entire unit at a therapeutic community meeting, he described his need to be cared for by staff on the unit:

If you really *cared*, then you would ask me how my day was . . . but you never ask . . . you don't *care*. I come onto the unit and ask how other people's . . . the staff's . . . day was, and all I get was, "mbmlskdmbl," because all you *care* about is leaving and going to your home. You really don't *care* about us here. We're just your job. That's all.

A second memory reflects a typical request for care in the residential units at this same hospital. During staff rounds, the young people were always eager to talk and play with the workers on the unit, especially in the early evening, when things were slow and boring. Whenever I entered a unit at this time of day, there were children who wanted to be hugged and asked how their day had gone. Others would ask, "Dr. Brett, do you want to play a game of air hockey?" And if my answer was no, I didn't have time, without fail I would hear, "If you *cared*, then you'd play with me." Feeling guilty, I would play the game because I wanted them to know I cared.

These young people teach us that care is important for all human beings, not only to make it through intolerably long days in hospitals, but to make it through life. Knowing that one is cared for and loved by others, and that one is able and has the chance to care for others, is especially important to children in psychiatric facilities, many of whom have been the victims of abuse and neglect.

What is care? This issue has been much debated by psychologists, educators, philosophers, and theologians. Harvard psychologist Carol Gilligan writes that the ideal of care is the activity of relationships, seeing and responding to the needs of others, taking care of the world by sustaining the web of connections so that no one is left alone.[2] Educator Nel Noddings believes that care is stepping out of one's personal frame of reference into another's life, with attention on the person being cared for and not on oneself.[3] Philosopher Milton Mayeroff argues that care only happens in relationships, where the caregiver moves away from his or her self to meet the needs of others.[4] Theologian Morton Kelsey believes that, in giving care, caregivers receive a sense of significant self-worth in life.[5]

While these abstract, theoretical definitions talk around the concept of care, they all fall short of capturing the essence of what care is, how we give and receive it, and why it is so important. Ben, an adolescent with behavioral problems, said it best during an assignment to draw a picture of love or care. He told me about the transcendent yet omnipresent nature of these two needs: "You can't draw freely that which is only felt between two people. Love is all around you; you can't see it because it is everywhere you are. It is so large you can't see it for what it really is."

Why is care so hard to define? Theologian Stanley Hauerwas understands that, by itself, unconnected with any other point of reference, the term *care* is ambiguous. Hauerwas rightly argues that care is a context-dependent term: the meaning of care is indefinite until specified within a particular context, often provided for by principles, roles, and institutions.[6] What helps us understand care is grounding it in the context of a story or, in this chapter, in the context of playing games with another person. For care may best be understood in the context and pattern of play and playing that we first learned as children in the backyard sandbox or on the playground swings.

Vivian Gussin Paley, an educator, writes that play establishes the context in which care and other lessons of life may be shaped and nurtured:

> Play and its necessary core of storytelling are the primary realities in the preschool and kindergarten, and they may well be the prototypes of imaginative endeavors throughout our lives. For younger students, however, it is not too much to claim that play contains the only set of circumstances understandable from beginning to end.[7]

It is in the act of playing games with other children that a child learns about many of life's emotions—by learning to win and lose, to forgive, and to care for one another. Play helps us solve the dilemmas of life and enables us to enjoy life. When I stop what I'm doing on a unit and pick up a paddle to play a quick game of Ping-Pong, I demonstrate that I care enough about the other person that I will stop what I'm doing to be with her or him. And I'm as gracious as I can be when my young opponent beats me.

To get a better understanding of what care is, and of its central importance in working, living, learning, and worshiping with children with disabilities, we need to look at it through the hermeneutic of play. The settings for our two examples of play and its relationship to care are both places for people whom society has labeled "disabled." The first narrative is from an ethnographic study of life in a l'Arche community in London, England. L'Arche is a Christian community for adults with mental retardation. The second example is from the Religious Narrative Project, which I have conducted with children who have emotional, behavioral, and developmental disabilities. In these two settings I have had firsthand experience of care in playing. And in these contexts I have come to appreciate the centrality of care for all people, regardless of abilities or limitations.

Considering Play in Understanding Care

We will look at ten characteristics of play and their direct implications for an understanding of care. This exploration exploring of care through the hermeneutic of play is an innovative way to gain new insight into an understanding of care. These ideas about care are also informed by two different sources, l'Arche and a private psychiatric hospital, both of which stress the act of caring in working and living with people with disabilities.

 1. *Play and care involve the self and another person.* The relationship between self and other is part of all playing. A machine can serve as the other, as in pinball or video games. Some would even argue that one can play against oneself, as the long-distance runner does when trying to beat a personal record. There is still something other than self that one is playing with or against.

 Like play, care involves the self and another person. In a setting such as a hospital or an institution for children with disabilities, the professional health-care worker assumes the role of caregiver, and the role of other is assumed by the taker or receiver of care. For example, at L'Arche Lambeth, assistants[8] are officially listed in the National Health Service of England as "care workers," or people whose primary job is to give care to persons with disabilities. The ethnographer Susan Foster, who conducted a study of an institution for people with mental retardation, writes that, in most institutions, there is an asymmetric dimension or "one-wayness" of care among the patients and the staff. It is assumed by many professionals that the care worker's job is to give care, and the patient's or resident's job is to receive care, *not* the other way around.[9]

But

Foster's observation of this asymmetric relationship between care worker and the one cared for holds true in both l'Arche and the setting with children. At l'Arche, one young assistant said that "care is looking over someone's shoulder and helping them when they're cooking and you're the one eating their food." Another assistant said that "care is looking after the concerns of someone else." A mental health technician, otherwise known as a frontline careworker, who works with the young children with disabilities, said, "Care is looking after the needs of someone else in a loving way."

2. *Play and care happen in the space between "me" and "not me."* Though there may be two players in a game, the real moment of play happens in between the players, in the interaction between the two. Play happens as the football is flying in the air and in the anticipation of a touchdown by one of the team players. Play is the surprisingly spontaneous laughter during charades or a silly board game. Play happens in a moment of time but cannot be frozen in time. The moment of play is dynamic and fleeting, sustained by the imagination and love of people in community.

Like play, care also happens in a moment, the moment between the giving and the taking, and sometimes in the sheer anticipation of caring for others or being cared for. Care happens in the very act of giving oneself to another who willingly receives the gift. Caring is action—a spontaneous back after a hard day; an unexpected gift on an ordinary day, a kind word from a co-worker out of the blue.

One of the "Mental Health Technicians" at the hospital said that care is located somewhere in the midst of the caring experience: "Care is experienced emotionally, spiritually, and naturally. It is an expression of love between two people . . . you can't touch it, yet it has gravity to it. It naturally happens as a part of being nurtured. When it happens, there is an overabundant sensation."

3. *Play and care are spontaneous, awakening what is good in all of us.* In play, we celebrate and dance close to the unknown of our lives, where the course of life's journey may change quickly and we may find ourselves suddenly on a new path. Games have that air of unpredictability. Who knows what we are going to do when engaged in a playful game? In essence, play describes best what the philosopher Alasdair MacIntyre said about human nature: human

beings are unpredictable. All we can predict about human beings is
that they are unpredictable.[10]

Care, like play, may also take place spontaneously between two
or more people, because we are unable to control what is going to
happen every moment in our lives or in the lives of others. Some of
our most caring moments, or moments when we received care, may
have come during the most spontaneous incidents in life. Very often in caring moments, even when we think we are sure how we
will act, we fool ourselves and react differently—meeting a caring
act with surprising laughter, for example, when tears might have
been expected.

At both l'Arche and the hospital, there have been times when
people who thought they were caregivers unexpectedly received
care from those being cared for. One day at the hospital, Dale, a
young man with emotional disabilities, took a walk with me, and
we talked about God's love and care for creation. Suddenly Dale
stopped in mid-stride to tell me that care is "having to love other
people *before* they love you." In in interview with a researcher at the
l'Arche community, Mark, a man with cerebral palsy, described
care as something that happens between assistants and the people
with disabilities in the houses. Then he stood up in the middle of
the interview and gave the researcher a firm hug.

4. *Play and care teach one stick-to-itiveness.* Inherent in the very
act of playing is a spirit of commitment in seeing a game through,
even when one is losing.[11] In the best spirit of sports, people encourage children and adults alike to at all times be "good sports," to
continue playing even when you know you're going to lose. There
is an unspoken code of ethics among players on winning teams
that calls on them to celebrate the efforts of players on both teams.
If a team is losing, there is an unwritten expectation that the players will continue to fight the good fight with all their might.

Care calls for this same spirit of commitment. In caring for a
person who is not always enjoyable to be around, there are moments when the idea or value of care as a commitment to another
person is borne out. L'Arche founder Jean Vanier has often said
that true community is that place where the person you least want
to live with always lives.[12] When that person moves away, someone
else arrives immediately to take his or her place.

Ben, at the center for children with disabilities, shares his perception of care in such terms of commitment:

Care is something or someone who will stick by you for a lifetime ... no matter what you might do to them, they still give you attention and love, like [your] parents, who put a roof over your head [and feed you].

5. *Play and care connect inner thoughts with outer actions.* Playing a game creates a context in which our inner thoughts and feelings can be revealed to others through our outer actions and responses. Some people are playful by nature, and they are seen by others as loving to play, as having a playful attitude. They enjoy playing with others because that context enables them to communicate their thoughts and feelings. This inner zest for life needs to have some outward expression. What is private needs, and is called, to be made public.

Just as some people are playful by nature, others are inherently caring. Their entire approach to life centers on caring for and about others. Like play, care calls one to share one's inner thoughts or attitudes into action. We know those who are called in this way by the way they are always asking about the other person rather than calling attention to themselves. They are the ones who remember birthdays and notice when someone gets a haircut. They remember the little details of other people's lives. Care is an outward expression, a conscious act to ensure the welfare, protection, or enjoyment of other people.

It is natural for the health professions to attract people who are naturally caring. Two assistants at l'Arche spoke eloquently about care as a connection between inner thoughts and outer actions. Caroline said: "Care becomes more than an attitude when tension and frustration flare up in your community; care becomes explicit when finding ways to bring peace in our community." For Pierre, care is a natural, internal gift: "Some people, because of what they've experienced in life, have the natural ability to care."

6. *Play and care take practice and experience.* We learn about the world and our relationship with others through play, but play requires practice.[13] To improve at play, people watch and observe oth-

ers' actions. They also practice, alone and with others. To be a good soccer or tennis player takes time, effort, and practice.

The act of caring also requires practice, even not hard work. Within each of us sometimes is something that does not want to care for others, but is tempted to sit by the wayside. This predisposition not to care makes it all the more important that we place ourselves in situations where we *have* to care. For it is caring for ourselves and others that either makes or breaks the human community.

Sociologist Robert Bellah, quoting the nineteenth-century French politician and writer Alexis de Tocqueville, observed this behavior of care in the United States: care is a custom, notion, opinion, and idea that "shapes mental habits" or is better understood as a "habit of the heart." Care involves not only ideas and opinions but also habitual practices with respect to such things as religion.[14] Care takes practice. Care *is* a practice, learned among a people whose lives are formed and sustained by the stories told and celebrated within a community.

At l'Arche, it is understood that care requires practice and hard work, that there is a practical dimension to caring. Phyllis, an assistant, said that care is "not letting Rud [a man who is mentally retarded] eat too much for his own good." Benjamin, another assistant, said that care is "demonstrated by how people are with the mentally handicapped, going through the hard times with others when you'd rather flee from them."

7. *Play and care are about self-renewal and re-creation.* We engage in play because it is truly enjoyable.[15] Even though some people may feel exhausted and tired after playing, most find that, in the long run, they feel better for having engaged in play, for the brief retreat from the rut of the routine. Play is life-giving because it provides a structure in a specific time and place and a reason for playing.[16] Play has its own special reason and logic that provides people a calming sense of security that allows people to release the pent-up emotions of the day. In play, people are able to let go of certain inhibitions and use their imaginations.

Care is also about self-renewal. Like play, care generates and invigorates life. The importance of caring for oneself by engaging in the act of playing was captured well by pastoral counselor Dr. Sandra Brown. Toward the end of a semester at a seminary, she would walk up to students who looked especially haggard from the stress of studying and ask, "When was the last time you played in the sand box of life? Perhaps you need to see a movie tonight."

Caring that is self-renewing occurs in the very act of giving and receiving care in the midst of community life. Alice, an assistant at l'Arche, said about care:

> If you care for others, you see that *you* have value and worth. There is the discovery of a new you, or a re-evaluation and discovery of self in the act of caring for, and being cared for by others.

8. *Play and care make us aware of our prejudices in life.* Many in the so-called men's movement see hidden role models and overgeneralized myths in America that men have used to define who they are in our culture. The man of the 1950s was supposed to like football, be aggressive, be patriotic, and never cry. The sixties man was confronted by women's history and sensibility and the idea of feminine consciousness. The seventies man is described as a "soft male," not interested in harming the earth or starting wars. The shifting ideals that shape the character of men in each decade are revealed in the very games men choose to play— football for the fifties male, for example, a game that epitomizes the aggressive posture of many men toward other people.[17]

As there are in play, there are situations in life when people find out not only how caring they can be, but also how careless and callous they can be. For example, the act of suicide makes many people painfully aware of how much and in what ways they have shown care for another person. When someone we thought we had cared for enough commits suicide, those left behind have to deal with the nagging question: "Did I care enough?"

It is often assumed that the role and function of an assistant or a mental health technician at l'Arche is to give care to another as "an object of care." It catches the care workers off-guard to be cared for by and receive care from those being cared for. Matthew, an assistant, said that new assistants at l'Arche always have difficulty receiving care from those with disabilities:

> Some new assistants don't want to receive care. Patrick, who is mentally handicapped, likes to give care . . . when he falls into the hands of an assistant who only *gives* and doesn't *receive* care, things get mucked up.

9. *Playing and caring are healing.* Playing a situation out is as therapeutic as talking out a problem, perhaps even more so.[18] Many play therapists will argue that play in the sandbox is full of meaning, that the scrawl on a pad of paper by a child's pen is telling us quite a bit about the "inner world" of the child. Many people play physical sports because doing so allows them a socially acceptable release for the tensions and frustrations of life.

Caring is as therapeutically healing for people as play is. In caring for other people, many caregivers find the care they had been missing in life. People who are depressed sometimes feel that no one cares for them, and this feeling deepens their depression. One way out of this depressive cycle may be to care for another person. People are hesitant to do this because they are convinced that care, or love, is a scarce resource—that they only have so much care to last a lifetime. They fear they'll use it all up. But the miracle of caring is that, the more we give, the more we receive, and the more we have to give,

For example, healing in the act of caring was manifest in the work projects at l'Arche when assistants wanted the people with disabilities to discover and then use their untapped gifts and talents. Kit, an assistant, described care as follows: "Care is challenging other people, trying to clear up misperceptions and inappropriate behaviors." Roger, also an assistant, said that care is "exploring the hidden gifts and talents of another, to flesh out . . . the gifts of another person while respecting the dignity and worth of the other; that's care."

10. *Play and care are the bridge between all people.* It is entertaining to see a multi-anything-and-everything group of people gather together in the act of playing. The whole purpose and philosophy

of *The New Games Book* is to identify games that link people who had no way to link up before, to engage their imaginations, and to have fun—all at the same time.[19] Play brings people together for joyous and harmonious interaction with others and the earth. In the act of playing together, a common ground emerges where all may have fun in life.

If the act of playing establishes a common ground between people, care is the glue that holds together the diversity of people in our world. It is because we care that people from different backgrounds join in the play of life. That is why individuals get involved in games: they care and enjoy the company of others. Care becomes the link, the nuts and bolts, the very tissue and sinew that allows people to play with one another.

The notion of care as connective in mutual relationships is prevalent at l'Arche. Sean, the director of l'Arche, said that care is a spirit of mutuality: "It exists in a mutual relationship that goes on between two or more people in caring. Care is the great equalizer in l'Arche." Care enables us to be with others in joy or to stay with someone in agony.

To Care Is to Play

Play and care go hand in hand. Both involve the interaction of people who know something about one another and desire to experience more of life together. Care is inherent in play. That's why parents take time to play with their children. And that's why all people, children and adults alike, take time to play. In the act of playing, we create a place for and a way of caring for one another.

Viewing care through the hermeneutic of play, we discover some implications for all caring professions. First, one way to begin a caring relationship is through play. If one plays long enough with another person, there is a chance that each player will move from seeing the other as an opponent to seeing the other as a person— someone to care for and to be cared about in return. The very character of the other person is revealed in the act of playing. Good play involves loving care, and loving care between two people involves play.

Second, caring and playing take concentrated effort and time. Good play and good care are a practice, a way of life, an ethic, that can get in the way of daily life. Just as in sports it is easier to be a poor loser than to be a good sport, in life it is easier not to care than to care. But to not play—to not care—would be less than human, if not actually inhumane.

Caring for people with disabilities—in hospitals, churches, or educational settings, is by no means cost-efficient, energy-saving, or predictable. But working with others in a caring manner is the most human way of living in a community devoted to the good that we hold in common—which, for those whose lives are centered in Christian faith, is God in Christ.

l'arche

A Caring Community

For over thirty years, l'Arche, a community of people with and without mental retardation, has become an important presence among both professional service providers and members of Jewish and Christian communities. As a community movement, l'Arche has stood outside traditional institutional circles of care, calling on professionals and laypeople to reconsider how we care for, educate, conduct therapy with, and *live* with people society has labeled "mentally retarded."

What is it that makes l'Arche what it is—an institution that now includes more than a hundred communities in both rich and poor countries? Having referred to l'Arche in other chapters, this chapter will explore some of what makes l'Arche a unique alternative for providing a permanent, caring home to persons with mental retardation. We will trace the history of this community and examine its theological assumptions. Then we will take a closer look at l'Arche, examining some of what I learned while doing a study there. Finally, we will discuss four characteristics of l'Arche that relate to quality-of-life issues.

The History of L'Arche Lambeth

L'Arche in the United Kingdom grew out of two separate movements in British society during the 1960s and 1970s. The first movement involved the proliferation of small, homelike Christian communities throughout Great Britain. Britain up until 1945 had been a nation of local communities, and people identified themselves primarily on the basis of where they lived. After World War II, with increased mobility, many families moved away from their hometowns, and there was a sense of communities breaking down, at least in terms of the way many people understood the term *community*. The parish church struggled to remain the social base of a stationary community, when in reality families were moving away all the time.[1]

Replacing the parish churches were small, alternative Christian communities, known in the 1960s as house churches, where people gathered for common activities, bringing forth the sense of significance, solidarity, or belonging once nurtured by the local congregation.[2] The church thus shifted from a community of place to a community of concern, and moved from formal worship and Sunday meetings to personal encounters with important world issues.

The second movement was the normalization and deinstitutionalization movement, started by a Dane named Niels Erik Bank-Mikklesen. The aim of this movement, which swept across Europe, was simple—to provide "the intellectually handicapped" with an everyday life and social environment that most closely resembled normal conditions.[3]

In 1980, a paper was published by the King's Fund Centre in England, an organization concerned with the well-being of persons with "mental handicaps." Titled "An Ordinary Life: Comprehensive Locally Based Residential Services for Mentally Handicapped People," this paper assumed three principles:

1. People with mental retardation have the same human value as anyone else and therefore the same human rights.
2. Living like others within a community is both a right and a need.
3. Services must recognize the individuality of those with mentally handicaps.

Based on these assumptions, "An Ordinary Life" called for a strategy to implement comprehensive community-based, residential services for people with mental retardation. The aim was to provide a comfortable, secure home and home life for people unable to find these on their own. Such homes were also to be places of education, of "doing and teaching," where residents could learn from trained staff who would help them become more independent in the business of everyday living.

The community that both embraced the nature of the alternative Christian "house church" and lived out the spirit of the "Ordinary Life" report was l'Arche. (The name means "ark," as in Noah's ark found in the book of Genesis.) Now a network of communities around the world where people with mental retardation live in homes with non-disabled persons, l'Arche was founded by two members of the Roman Catholic church. Jean Vanier, a theologian and philosopher from Canada, began l'Arche, with the help and encouragement of a priest named Father Thomas, in the small French village of Trosly-Breuil. Father Thomas had been working with a group of adult men with mental retardation in a small institution in this village when he asked Vanier to join him in caring for these men.

Vanier created l'Arche

in the desire to live the gospel and to follow Jesus Christ more closely. Each day brings me new lessons on how much Christian life must grow in commitment to life in community, and on how much that life needs faith, the love of Jesus, and the presence of the Holy Spirit if it is to deepen.[4]

In this spirit, he asked two men with mental retardation, Phillipe and Raphael, to move into his house, which he named l'Arche. Vanier's experience with these men elicited for him a new image of people with disabling conditions, helping him see the intrinsic value of all human life that can emerge when people with disabilities live in community with those who are non-disabled.

L'Arche Lambeth, a l'Arche community located in the London district of Lambeth, is home to more than fifty people, twenty-one of whom are mildly to moderately mentally retarded; the other thirty are non-disabled residents, known as "assistants." Begun in 1977, l'Arche Lambeth was the fourth l'Arche community in the

United Kingdom (the others are in Kent, Liverpool, and Inverness). L'Arche Lambeth was started by Jean Vanier's sister, Therese Vanier, who also began the Kent community. With the help of interested people in the Lambeth area, a house called "the Vine" was found for l'Arche. Five people who were mentally retarded were invited to come to the Vine from St. Lawrence's, a government-sponsored institution for people with mental retardation on the outskirts of south London. Five assistants also moved into the house. The funds for this community were raised with the help of the Board of Trustees of St. Thomas' Hospital in London. Since that time, the community has grown to include four more houses, a workshop called the Wedge, and a half-acre garden plot.

How does l'Arche grow and recruit new assistants? Two of l'Arche Lambeth's first assistants came to the community through what has become a fairly typical pattern. Having heard of l'Arche through friends, they read some of the works of Jean Vanier and heard him speak. Sean and Sarah,[5] a married couple, were two of the first to support this fledgling community:

> In 1976, there was the creation of a Faith and Sharing retreat which Jean Vanier gave in Birmingham, and we were able to go to that. I think that it was during that time that we learned that there was the possibility of a l'Arche community in Lambeth. . . . Later on, we were involved in a holiday group with the other l'Arche communities of Inverness and Kent.

Along with Therese Vanier, and Pierre from the Little Brothers of Jesus (a community of Catholic laymen started in France), l'Arche Lambeth opened its doors in welcome to five adults—Mark, Penelope, Delia, George, and another Mark.

Many of those with disabling conditions came to l'Arche Lambeth through Lambeth Social Services, which recommended people in the Lambeth area who would be a good fit for the community. George, one of the men with mental retardation, remembers hearing of l'Arche from his mother: "She said, 'It'd be a good idea for you, George. You'd learn a lot of things.' And now it's my home." All who come to l'Arche stay for a probationary period of one month, to see whether the arrangement will work. After six months, l'Arche reviews each probationary resident's case and decides whether to "extend an invitation" to become a permanent part of the community. Once the invitation has been offered and accepted, the community is considered the person's home for life.

The Theology of l'Arche

Jean Vanier believes that l'Arche communities are grounded in the gospel of Jesus Christ, a belief emphasized in the rituals of the evening prayers in each l'Arche house. Three central ideas that support l'Arche theologically are (1) covenant and a sense of belonging; (2) growth and nourishment; and (3) the gifts each person has to share. All three are based on God as revealed in the person of Jesus Christ. These ideas are best stated in the Beatitudes, or the Sermon on the Mount (see Matt. 5:1–12; Luke 6:17, 20–23), where we read, "Blessed are the poor, for theirs is the dominion of God" (Luke 6:20b). It was in these words that Jean Vanier found a message that has truly inspired community to happen, a community that includes those whom the world considers poor—people with mental retardation.[6]

Covenant and Belonging

Vanier writes that there is a covenant between Jesus and the poor.[7] This is why L'Arche has welcomed those with mental retardation—because they are the poor in our world community. A community is only a community when the majority of its members have consciously decided to break down barriers reach out to enemies or to those who are poor.[8] In reaching out to the poor, we learn how to live the gospel. That is why those who are poor are considered the treasures of the church.

The function of the community, built on this covenant with those who are poor, is to provide a loving and secure place where people in need may find a "home." It is into a home that l'Arche welcomes those who are disabled, not because these people are necessarily Christian, but because they are lonely and distressed. Only in community, in a mutual, caring relationship with others, can a person find a sense of belonging and a place he or she can call "home."

Growth and Nourishment

A community is on a journey of life and faith, with two frailties: the weakness of birth and the dependence of one who is dying. And that growth journey is a movement toward integration of our deep self with our strengths and weaknesses, our riches and our poverty.[9] But in that journey there will be times of trial and tension, bringing the whole community to face its own poverty and its inability to cope with the tensions of life. What finally pulls the community through is the awareness that it needs the spirit of God in order to live and grow.

That sense of deepening growth comes from nourishment. The essential nourishment is fidelity to the thousand and one small demands of each day, the effort to live and forgive "the enemy," and to welcome and accept community structures—and all this comes by way of cooperation with authority. This fidelity is based on the belief that Jesus has called people to this covenant with the poor, our brothers and sisters. For it is Jesus who has called us to love and who will accompany us and give us strength.

Gifts

Vanier has written that a community is like an orchestra: each instrument produces a beautiful sound when it is played alone, but when all the instruments are played together, each given its own weight, the result is even more beautiful.[10] To love others is to recognize their gifts and to help them use and strengthen those gifts. A community is beautiful when all its members can use their talents fully. In this orchestra of life, those who have been called "disabled" play an essential part in the community.

We have seen what is important in Jean Vanier's Christian vision of life in community. But what is the vision of life held by those who live in a l'Arche community—both the assistants and those who are mentally retarded?

A Closer Look at l'Arche

To learn what makes a living community like l'Arche work, I felt it was important to experience its daily rhythm of life firsthand, from cooking meals to taking trips around England with other members of the community. I listened to conversations, took notes, and collected life histories. From twenty members of the community—ten persons with mental retardation and ten assistants—I also collected information through questionnaires and interviews. Their responses reflected their perspectives on friendship, trust, care, the role of rituals, and the language of l'Arche.

The four characteristics I focused on in my study of l'Arche were community, trust, care, and friendship.

Community

Sean, the director of l'Arche Lambeth, describes community as a common ground or meeting place where those with differences can gather and live together. As a common ground for people with differences, the community also serves some other important roles and functions in for both those with disabling conditions and the assistants.

Community is living and working together. Beatrice and George, two l'Arche members with mental retardation, see community as the place they both live and work for their living: "It is a place where we live and work together with assistants."

Community is belonging. While many said that community meant living together, another assistant said it could also mean "a set of people not living together, [yet still having] a sense of responsibility for each other, as in this community." Matthew, an assistant in charge of finances, believes community is "belonging, pure and simple." Fulfilling a need for belonging makes l'Arche work for many assistants.

Community is a home that works like a family. Alice, a house leader, feels that community works like a family. Another assistant believes that community is "an enlarged family, and living with the nitty gritty of life." Pierre, a workshop assistant, couldn't see how people could live outside a community. It was basic to being human.

Trust

Sociologist Randall Collins has written that communities and societies are based on trust, which makes it possible for people to live and work closely together without worrying about being taken advantage of. Trust makes people want to contribute to a friendship and to a community rather than protect only their own self-interests.[11] Anthropologist Mary Douglas affirms the centrality of trust in a community, stating that "anyone who has accepted trust and demanded sacrifice or willingly given either knows the power of the social bond of trust."[12] L'Arche believes that trust is essential to the success of its communities.

Trust is a need in the community. Most assistants see trust as an integral part of community life. At some point or another in our lives, all people have to trust others in order to survive.

Trust is a fragile virtue. Sean and Alice said that trust needs to be worked on, because it is something learned and something that can be lost. Trust is also a matter of luck. One assistant believes that one has to "be careful or lucky with trust. I haven't had a broken trust with people here because I've learned from other communities. You have to pick whom you want to talk to about any problems, plans, ambitions, or criticisms." Melody, a house leader, sees trust for the daily activities in community. She senses that sometimes "there isn't a great deal of trust in l'Arche. There is a small group of people who have so much control and say that people are afraid to let go and trust in l'Arche. I wonder if it is healthy or unhealthy. If community is a group of people with equal say, that's not happening here."

Trust is a part of friendship. Many assistants made a connection right away between trust and friendship. Caroline, an assistant at the Vine, was eloquent in her description of trust:

Trust and friendship are connected—very much so. Hand in hand, they are: the more I trust someone, the closer I'll be to that person, open up, without being terrified of who I am.

Trust is not something built up automatically. Trust in relationships can be shaken and diminish because trust is a lively thing. And it is so important to be open and honest, and trustful towards self and others.

Trust is a necessity for people with mental retardation. Because those with mental retardation have little choice but to place their trust in the goodwill of the assistants, assistants generally agree that trust is very important between staff and those who are mentally retarded. Phyllis, a house assistant at the Elmstone, said:

> Trust has to play a large part. The handicapped have to put a lot of trust in us. They have to do what we say. The pressure is on the handicapped to trust us. It's not always good. It's unbalanced trust, but that's the way it is.
>
> The mentally handicapped have to trust us out of necessity. Rud [who is mentally retarded] has to trust me after my being here for only a week.

Care

Philosopher Milton Mayeroff has written that caring plays two important roles in human life. First, caring helps others to grow and realize their potential. A child grows when her parent respects her independent existence and need to grow. Second, caring gives order and meaning to the life of a community. By caring for others and serving them, we live out the meaning of our lives. Milton Mayeroff says that community itself is "most at home in the world through caring and being cared for."[13] Care is a central value in the l'Arche community.

Care is an attitude. Pierre feels that care is an intuitive gift. He describes care in l'Arche as "an attitude of concern beyond oneself. Some people, because of what they've experienced, have the natural ability to care for others."

Care is solidarity with one another. Pierre describes care as solidarity—"the realization that we aren't achieving only for ourselves." For Alice, care is working alongside people with mental retardation who can care for themselves: "Disabled people can often care for self and others. If you care for others, you see that you have value and worth." Sean also said that care is standing with the other person, existing in a "mutual relationship [that] goes [on] between people in caring. Care in l'Arche is equal between the mentally handicapped and assistants."

Care is responding to need. Many assistants that feel care is best demonstrated by responding to the needs of others and giving care in l'Arche. Caroline believes that care is not only responding to others' needs but anticipating those needs, as in asking someone if she wants butter on their bread *before* she asks. Roger, a workshop assistant, believes that caring for others is challenging them to explore their hidden talents—"knowing that [those with mental retardation] have latent gifts that need to be plumbed out, and then respecting the other person." But in challenging them, he also understands that care means "sticking around" out of a commitment to seeing the task through.

Care is receiving and giving assistance. Delia, who is mentally retarded, said that, "Around my house [the assistants] give me clothes and everything." Maggie, who has epilepsy, talked about "being cared for by crossing the road. Sometimes I fall."

Some people with mental retardation not only receive care but also give it. Mark, a man with cerebral palsy and mental retardation, told me about care, then he came over, gave me a hug, and said, *"That's* care. All right?" Dennis, a young man with cerebral palsy, showed care for others in his house: "I look after [the assistants], I do. Give them tea sometimes." Matthew, a house assistant, feels new assistants often have a hard time because they believe they have to care for others all the time:

> Some [assistants] don't want to receive care. Patrick, who is mentally handicapped, likes to give care. . . . When we fall into the assistants only *giving* care, things get mucked up around here.

Friendship

Philosopher Alasdair MacIntyre has written that friendship is one person's well-wishing and well-doing out of concern for the other person's good, which "is essential and primary to the constitution of any form of community, whether that of a household or that of a city."[14] Friendship may also be understood as sharing with others a moral or ethical commitment.[15] Friendship is central to the life of l'Arche, and there are examples in many of the relationships in a l'Arche community. Rud and Dave, two men with mental retardation at the Elmstone, sit together at supper and walk together to the workshop every day, not leaving the house until the other is ready. People describe friendship in l'Arche in various terms.

Friendship is a necessity. All of the assistants interviewed think that friendship is an important need in the life of the community, a key to living together. Some believe that everyone at l'Arche is their friend, while others perceive friendship as a scarce but much-needed commodity. One assistant said, "There's a need to share with somebody, a mirror, of what is happening in my life in l'Arche."

Friendship is a choice. Friendship in a l'Arche community does not always happen automatically. One assistant said, "Sometimes you naturally click with someone, and you don't click with all of the people, even among the handicapped." A similar thought was echoed by Matthew:

> Not everyone is a friend in l'Arche. You need to work at friendship. It's easy to be lonely. I remember a house where I didn't have any friends in it. I wasn't naturally drawn towards others.

"Everyone's my friend" at l'Arche. Many people who are mentally retarded believe that friends are important. That universalization of friendship is a common perception among those with disabling conditions. Hugging each other, Bea and George said, "*Everyone* is my friend." Only one person with mental retardation told me that some people "really annoy me in l'Arche."

The Growing Edges—and Growing Pains—of L'Arche Lambeth

While l'Arche holds out new hope and many promises for a fuller life for people who are mentally retarded and the assistants who live with them, a number of important issues challenge the community to grow. Jean Vanier himself makes it very clear that no one thinks or dreams that l'Arche *is* the dominion of God on earth. L'Arche is having to confront the pains of growing older, growing larger, and becoming more established in countries throughout the world. Three issues facing l'Arche are: (1) a split between assistants and those with mental retardation, (2) the recognition of those who are mentally retarded as whole persons, and (3) the burnout of young assistants.

The Split between the Two Groups in l'Arche

Despite their commitment to the alternative kind of care l'Arche provides, the assistants I interviewed would often slip into identifying others according to their condition, thereby creating a kind of "we-they" relationship. What emerges in the innocent act of labeling people in l'Arche is a quality of sameness, reinforced by the institutional structure of the community. L'Arche struggles to find ways of talking about its two groups of people, those with and those without disabilities, without implying that either group is homogenous.

Getting Older

Jean Vanier told me that when he took Raphael and Philippe into his home in Trosly, he believed this act was irreversible: they could never return home or to the institution, for his home was now their home.

As l'Arche has grown older, so have the people within its communities. The young assistants who came with a common vision of l'Arche, who committed their lives to living in l'Arche, are now older, and in some cases, close to the age of retirement. Many issues concerning retirement and traditional benefit packages are arising. Those with mental retardation are also growing older. Many communities provide workshop settings for younger members, but l'Arche is increasingly having to provide geriatric care for its people.

Recruiting and Keeping Assistants

Just as in other settings for people with disabling conditions, the standard, routine schedule and seemingly slow learning pace of those who are mentally retarded often leads to exhaustion among many assistants. Many leave after only one year.

What is interesting about this turnover of assistants is that it makes it clear whose home l'Arche really is. In my study, I asked both assistants and those with mental retardation an innocuous question: Where is home for you? Invariably, the assistants responded with the name of the community where they'd been raised—Derbyshire, York, Boston. Every one of the people with mental retardation gave the name of their l'Arche community: the Vine, the Mustard Seed, the Elmstone, the Sycamore House. When I returned to l'Arche Lambeth three years later, many of the assistants had left the community, while all those with mental retardation were still there. It was, is, and will be in the foreseeable future *their* community and home. They are the community historians, the keepers of the traditions, rituals, and stories of the many people who have crossed the threshold of their homes.

L'Arche: A Community That Cares

What is so unique about l'Arche that people from all over the world continue to live in these communities where the pay and benefits are minimal compared with other institutions? Few group homes and institutions for people with mental retardation in this world attract such global interest and participation.

One explanation may be that, whereas conventional secular institutions purport to be team-based, resident-centered communities where virtues of trust, care, and friendship are important, hardly anyone talks about and tries to live these virtues on a regular basis. These virtues are not part of their day-to-day vocabulary. In l'Arche communities, on the other hand, the language and gestures of community are explicitly discussed, prayed about, and practiced daily as central ingredients of community life. The importance of such values—along with the biblically based, Christian virtues of faith, hope, and love—is continually brought forth in readings, writings, and discussions within l'Arche communities.

Second, many secular institutions fail to see that trust is fragile, and the damage that results when trust is not honored can be so devastating that it can destroy cooperation within an organization or community.[16] This affects not only administration of the facility, but the very care and well-being of those who are there for treatment. At l'Arche, trust is the bond that keeps the community members together, with an almost religious zeal.

Third, instead of embracing the dynamics of *mutual* care, many secular institutions place a high value on controlling the behaviors of residents. In these institutions, care is usually one-way, directed only from the care worker to the one who is disabled. In l'Arche communities, the care of people attempts to go in both directions. Little if any behavioral programming is used in l'Arche, even with those who are considered to be severely or profoundly mentally retarded. Most of the care focuses on the uniqueness of those with disabilities and how they interact with others and the world. This approach brings out the best in all those living in l'Arche and provides a resource of healing in love and respect for self and others.

Finally, secular institutions focus on self-control, self-growth, and self-esteem, with a spotlight on the "self" rather than on relationships. In many institutions, there is little emphasis on the responsibility one has for others in caring, trusting friendships. Because l'Arche is firmly grounded in the sacred story of the Christian faith, it recognizes the primacy of relationships as the way to care for others. For this is the way of Jesus Christ.

Just as Jesus identified so closely with those who were visibly wounded, proclaiming that God's healing good news is for them, Jean Vanier and those who have participated in his vision sense a closeness to God in living and working for those who are mentally retarded. The continuing manifestation of God's presence in the lives of those who have been devalued by society has called, and continues to call, faithful people to be part of this community that cares.

chapter fifteen

the unexpected
community

Like many experiences of Christian community, people only know that they have experienced this kind of community *after* it has happened.

Consider the drama and comedy that unfolded at the Montreat Conference Center, a Christian conference for families in the mountains of western North Carolina, where five families with children with disabilities were attending a conference. The children with disabilities attended a full-day camp program for three days. As they would be in school, the children were assigned to groups according to their ages and grades. Each disabled child was accompanied by an older adolescent who could provide assistance if needed. These "Best Buddies" were members of church youth groups who were present at the retreat center as part of a mission project.

On the last day of the conference, the disabled children gathered together with their parents and their Best Buddies to share stories of their experiences during the week at camp. The Montreat Conference Center hosts this closing-day gathering in the form of an "Ice Cream Cone Social," and I had an opportunity to witness the happy melee, complete with dozens of dripping ice cream cones.

The interaction of the children with disabilities with their family members and their Best Buddies was amazing to watch. There was Eddy,[1] a blonde, blue-eyed, eight-year-old who had mental retardation and attention deficit disorder (ADD) due to fetal alcohol syndrome. Eddy delighted in hugging people unexpectedly, then running away before anyone could hug him back. Seven-year-old Joy, who also had ADD, seemed to be in heaven, smiling and giggling infectiously with the Best Buddies who were a bit winded from trying to catch her all week. Fifteen-year-old Laurie Ann, with mental retardation and cerebral palsy, was trying hard to get into every photograph being taken by the young people. Then there was red-haired Ruth, four years old, with mental retardation and cerebral palsy. With ice cream melting down her front and onto her communication board, she was grinning from ear to ear. Though Ruth was non-verbal, her smile and tinkling laughter told everyone present that all was right with her world. And there was the pudgy three-year-old, Mary, sitting on the ground. Mary, who had epilepsy, was focusing all her attention on the task of finishing her scrumptious ice cream before going home.

At this gathering, an unexpected community began to take form, a community that affected our lives in wonderful ways. The youth group members, who had given a week of their summers to be Best Buddies, talked about the rapid and unanticipated changes that had taken place in their young, still malleable lives. They all claimed to see children with disabilities differently now. A bond between the youth group members and the children was beginning to evolve. These adolescents, who had had no previous training in special education, were amazed by how attached they had become to the children in such a short time. They admitted that when they had first met these "strange kids," they'd been nervous about the demands that would be placed on them. But now they were busy hugging and photographs of the children, saying goodbye, and thanking one another for a week of rich memories.

The parents of the children with disabilities were also part of this hive of activity. They seemed amazed at their mixed feelings at the end of this week. Being a parent of a child with a disability is always a perplexing mix of conflicting emotions and dilemmas. A parent once told me that living with her daughter with a disability was sometimes like a sweet-and-sour American-Chinese dish: providing care for a disabled child can be both sweet and sour, both joy and burden. But this had been a week of respite care for the parents, a week where someone else had taken over the joys and burdens of caring for their children.

Joy's father thanked the youth group for the care they had provided his daughter. Mary's mother, Lolly, said that—had it not been for the conference—she didn't think her family would have had any vacation that summer. Then she broke into tears of thankfulness. Eddy's father spoke eloquently to the adolescent Best Buddies about his family's assumption that they wouldn't have a break from Eddy this summer, and what an unexpected surprise this had been. From this deep sharing, with youth group members and parents giving thanks, everyone knew that God had just moved through our midst. We were witnessing the creation and sustaining power of an unexpected community of Christian love.

Some of the lessons learned from participating in this unexpected community were:

1. The children with disabilities had three days in camp programs where they had the opportunity to play with other children their age. They participated in arts and crafts, hikes, and swimming— just as other children in the program.
2. The youth group members learned something about the radical nature of love as charity. They learned that blessings of this kind of love are evoked only when practiced in sharing it with others in community.
3. The parents' needs—for rest and respite care—were provided for in ways that they did not expect that week, which truly made the experience a rich gift to them.

Looking back, I see that a community was formed as needs were met in a mysteriously, somewhat serendipitous fashion. What made this all the more dramatic and joyous for those gathered at the ice cream social was the fact that this experience of Christian community was not something that anyone present had experienced recently in the context of their home parishes or congregations, at least not on such a dramatic scale. For many of those present, their children with disabilities had not been readily received into their home church's weekly programs. Some of the children had been placed in special Sunday school classes and not permitted to join in the other, age-appropriate classes. Because of their disabilities, some of the children present had not been welcomed into the worship service of a congregation, and neither were other members of their families. Some of the families had encountered pastors who made it clear that children with disabilities were not to come front for the children's sermon because of their possible "disruptive behaviors."

These inhospitable acts had driven some of the familes away from church. For many, church had become a place where only "normal" people could worship their "normal" God, not a welcome place for all people, especially those with disabilities.

What these children with disabilities did at the Retreat Center was call us together into being Christian community. Without their presence, we strangers (none of us had known each other before coming to Montreat) would not have become a community. These children shocked even their own parents into recognizing that they—children with disabilites that some churches considered "disruptive"—were called to be part of a Christian community. We were witnesses to God's grace breaking into our ordinary experiences, an extraordinary moment of community.

The metaphor that may best explain what happened is found in Romans 12, where the apostle Paul describes the church as a body, the members of which are given life by the gift of God's grace. Biblical scholar Günther Bornkamm wrote about this passage that no one is without a gift. In this body, no matter how different the form that gift takes from person to person, the effect of grace is in every case concrete.[2] Theologian Karl Barth echoes this sentiment when he says that we can know our place in this body only in the interaction that the members of this body have among one another. It is in the sharing, the encounters with one another, the give-and-take of life's experiences, that the members of the body perceive that they are part of *the* fellowship with God.[3]

That there are various parts to Christ's body is key to this passage from Romans. The apostle Paul expresses the various gifts found in this body, which are to be shared by specific actions, certain gestures: "Prophecy, in proportion to faith; ministry, in ministering; the teacher, in teaching; the exhorted, in exhortation; the giver, in generosity; the leader, in diligence; the compassionate, in cheerfulness" (Rom. 12:6–7). *All* are important; none should be taken for granted.

What was clear at this moment of community was that we were called together, pulled together, from our busy and often self-centered lives, by the presence of these non-traditional ministers of God. These very children, whom many would classify as the "least of these" or the "less respectable members" in the body of Christ, are truly gifted evangelists. These children with disabilities were active participants in calling their parents, their Best Buddies, and this observer—all of whom had been strangers to one another—into a community of Christian love as members of the body of Christ. We were drawn out of our isolation into a community of friends in Christ.

The name of the gift that these children brought to the forefront of our undivided attention was the gift that the apostle Paul calls the "greater gift"—love as charity. This "higher," or "greater" gift is essential for the overall welfare of the Church. In 1 Corinthians 12, Paul wrote that we should all "strive for the greater gifts. And I shall show you a still more excellent way"—the way of love.

In the transparency of human emotions being shared, where laughter and tears were intermingling, a memory of Christian community was planted in our lives. The parents left hoping that they could come back to this moment again. The youth group members went back to their respective churches far richer for having been with others who have much to teach us about the wildness of God's mercy. And the children with disabilities went home having discovered new friends. Much diversity there is in this gift of the unexpected community, the one body of Christ.

chapter sixteen

the politics of dis/abilities

The Nation-State's Politics of Independence versus the Church's Politics of Dependence

An advertisement for *Mouth: The Voice of Disability Rights* makes the audacious claim that this new publication takes a

> clear-eyed, realistic stance that disability is a political rather than a personal (read "private") issue, and that most of the do-gooders and so-called helping professionals are just so many impediments to a life of independence and self-respect . . . or as one writer put it in an issue about the myth of rescue, "I know now that when I hear the words 'we're here to help you,' it's a warning to run—not walk—in the opposite direction."[1]

It was the line that a "disability is a political rather than personal issue" that rang true for me.[2] I have written and said such things many times, but perhaps not with the same clarity and honesty. Of course, a disability is whatever a particular group of people defines as a disability. In other words, every disabling condition is a cultural invention or social construction rather than a personal or private problem. Whether one is called "handicapped" or "disabled," "mentally retarded" or "developmentally delayed" is determined by some group of people, which in the United States is usually the Congress. When we understand that politics, or the *polis,* is the place where people share a vision of the human good that will define some type of community, we see that all disabilities are a matter of politics. Our perception of a handicapping condition, and our corresponding definition of what is or is not a disability, is determined by the location (or context) in which that politic is practiced by a certain group of people. The location where a politic is practiced matters a lot, just as location matters a great deal in real estate. *Who* is disabled in a culture is determined by *which* politics the culture practices and the history and location of *where* it is practiced.

I intend to explore the politics of dis/abilities in general, and *competing* politics of disabilities in particular—namely, the politics of the nation-state versus the politics of the church. More precisely, I will highlight the differences in the politics practiced in what is commonly understood to be the civic government, the politics practiced by those empowered to define "disability," and the politics practiced in the church. For the politics practiced in the nation-state has turned out to be anything but a friend to the common good when that which is common includes people with disabilities. This chapter will show how disability groups have therefore created their own agenda, centered on their disability.

The other politic of dis/abilities we will explore is that of the church, which is, at the best of times, somewhat disabled as it appears to be arthritic and caught in spastic fits and starts and momentary collapse. But the church may be the only thing that saves many people considered disabled from atrophy, if not death. Indeed, the church, the body of Christ, may have to explicitly proclaim itself a sanctuary and become a place of safekeeping, practicing the gestures of God's mercy for people considered disabled, because of their treatment in an increasingly heartless world.

Politics of the Nation-State: Friend or Foe to People with Disabilities?

The philosopher Alasdair MacIntyre writes that the politics of the nation-state, as described by Aristotle, have been romanticized into a vision of a nation as a potential community whose unity can be expressed through the institution of the nation-state. This is the nation-state as an all-embracing community held together by a shared vision of the human good, with practices that shape a people to uphold this common good.[3]

Beginning in the 1950s, and continuing through the 1970s, people with disabilities were taken quite seriously by the nation-state we call the United States. In the 1950s, through what was then the Association of Retarded Children, programs for children and adults with disabilities were booming. In the 1960s, with deinstitutionalization and the hope of community mental health centers, people with disabilities were no longer locked behind institutional fences; they were coming back home. In the 1970s, we welcomed children and adults with disabilities into educational programs once reserved for "normal" people. "Mainstreaming" and "integration" were (and still are) the catchwords for that educational approach.

Finally, in the latter part of the 1980s, the Americans with Disabilities Act was signed into law, and people with disabilities were granted the same civil rights as any other "oppressed minority." People with all kinds of disabilities truly came to believe they had independence, free choice, and the power of the vote, thus making them a political constituency. "People First" became the cry of self-advocates with mental retardation. "We are no longer disabled; just call our culture 'DEAF,'" signed people who were hard of hearing and deaf. No longer was it the "Association of Retarded Children" or even "Retarded Citizens," but simply "The Arc." "I am physically challenged, not handicapped," proclaimed the bumper sticker on the back of a wheelchair. "I've got Ups syndrome," read the T-shirt of a young girl with a chromosomal anomaly, the word "Down's" defiantly crossed out.

In the 1990s, however, a sometimes subtle, often drastic change has taken place in the relationship between the nation-state and people with disabilities. Even while President Bush was signing the Americans with Disabilities Act, and the nation-state appeared to be an advocate for people with disabilities and their families, the economics of caring for and treating people with disabilities started to have an adverse effect, not only on programs for these people, but on their very lives. Alasdair MacIntyre has called the nation-state "a dangerous and unmanageable institution, presenting itself on the one hand as a bureaucratic supplier of goods and services, which is always about to, but never actually does, give its clients value for money."[4] For families of children with disabilities, as well as those with disabilities themselves, just when they have become dependent on the nation-state, not only for goods and services but also for certain "inalienable rights" and money for services and programs, it looks more and more as if the nation-state is not a friend after all.

One can see how the individualistic, market-driven philosophical ideals of the Enlightenment have shaped our notion of living with people with disabilities in the phenomena of the Individualized Education Plan (IEP), the Human Genome Project, and the recent Americans with Disabilities Act.

The Individualized Education Plan (IEP)

One of the "gifts" of the Enlightenment, especially in the manifestation of capitalism, was removing from a person any responsibility or accountability to others. Before the Enlightenment, a person was considered part of a complex web of relationships; with the birth of the "self," individuals became free to make up their own mind, without family, friends, or even the church to help shape and nurture them in the cultural practices into which they were born. This freedom, this independence from relationships, means being one's own authority in matters concerning one's life.

Independence and individuality are part and parcel of programs for people with disabilities. In schools, the nation-state provides the grand experiment called the Individualized Education Plan (IEP), which helps to remind people who work with disabled individuals that all people with a particular disability are not the same, nor should they be educated in the same way. But what is lost is a sense of this person having a past, present, or future—a narrative or biographical vantage point. Most IEPs deal in the present, with little regard for the storied context we are all part of. Furthermore, most IEPs fail to consider that the person is part of a larger, more significant community of relationships.

One's disability or limitation is not a personal or private affair. Rather, as any parent of a child with a disability will tell you, a disability involves a whole family, a whole church, a whole neighborhood. With a disability, there is no independence. The question is not whether persons who are disabled are dependent or independent, but rather, who do they depend on?

Misplaced Faith in Science: The Human Genome Project

One proposed alternative to faith in God, especially in the context of children being born with what society has determined to be disabilities, is whether something can be done medically to find a "cure." Better yet, is there any way, besides abortion, that we can solve the riddle of genetics and thereby genetically prevent the possibility of any child being born with "defects"? Which genes do we consider "disabled" or "deviant"?

Andrew Kimbrell, in his book *The Human Body Shop*, explores the eugenics movement both in the United States and in Nazi Germany, as well as its incarnation in the present decade, the Human Genome Project. The word *eugenics*, which comes from a Greek word meaning "nobly or well born," was first used by Sir Francis Galton in 1883. Galton wanted to ensure that the more "suitable race or strain of blood be given a better chance of prevailing speedily over the less suitable," which included not only people with disabilities, but also the "unfavored races of humans," such as anyone who wasn't white.[5] The eugenics movement included negative eugenics, which prevented the "unfit" (those viewed as "insane, feebleminded, criminal or in any other way inferior") from propagating, while the more aristocratic, superior traits were to be encouraged.[6] In 1896, Connecticut became the first state to regulate marriage for breeding purposes. The law provided that "no man and woman either of whom is epileptic, or imbecile, or feeble minded" shall marry or have extramarital relations "when the woman is under forty-five years of age."[7] Later, people with disabilities, the "unfit," were sterilized, first for their own good, and later for the good of the nation-state. Such eugenics was soon practiced not only in the United States, but throughout Canada and Europe, including Nazi Germany.

The new eugenics is found in the Human Genome Project, which started in 1959 with the identification of chromosomal anomalies responsible for Down's syndrome. With the discovery of the causes of sickle-cell anemia and other single-gene hereditary disorders, a new revolution had begun. The $3-billion Human Genome Project, which the U.S. government partially funds, is designed to decipher all of the more than 100,000 genes in the human body. This will enable doctors to screen fetuses and test-tube embryos for an extraordinary variety of physical and behavior traits. One scientist commented, "We should be able to locate which combinations affect kinky hair, olive skin, and pointy teeth." People would be able to decide which children they wanted to bear and could discard those seen as imperfect or defective.[8] This is clearly eugenics, though we don't give it that name. It gives people the ability to determine not only *when* to have children and *how many*, but also *what kind* of children.

Does science—or, more precisely—do scientists bear a grudge toward people with disabilities? Consider the story of Sandra Jensen, a thirty-four-year-old woman with Down's syndrome, who was denied a life-sustaining heart-lung operation (the same one Mickey Mantle had). The reason? Because, a spokesperson for Stanford University Medical Center said, "We do not feel that patients with Down's syndrome are appropriate candidates for heart-lung transplantation." Although Sandra could pay the $250,000 for the transplant, it was initially denied her because she is mentally retarded.

Sandra Jensen's situation is not unusual. Thanks to such books as *The Bell Curve*, which favors abandoning government programs that offer assistance to people based on race, persons determined to have low IQ scores are doomed to failure. Ethicist Peter Singer proposed that there be a twenty-eight-day period in which parents and doctors could choose infanticide to end a "life that has begun very badly"—a life that includes Down's syndrome, for example. Dorothy Nelkin, who wrote *The DNA Mystique*, states that research such as the Human Genome Project offers the "promise" of controlling disease and disability, with a "rising stigma attached to people believed to be genetically predisposed to be less competent."[9]

The Americans with Disabilities Act: A Handicapped Act

In 1990, President George Bush, with a host of church and federal leaders surrounding him, signed the Americans with Disabilities

Act. The law was proclaimed as the "civil rights law for people with disabilities." The questions raised after the ADA was signed and the small print was read, however, dared to ask exactly who was being served and managed by this legislation, and how long—or, more precisely—how short were the arms of this law.

To begin with, the number of people with disabilities was set at 43 million, a number that does not include people with learning disabilities, certain mental illnesses, or even AIDS or HIV. There are approximately 120 million more persons with disabilities in the United States, if you count all diseases and chronic health conditions. Thirty-one million people have arthritis, for example, but the condition limits only 7 million. So who does the ADA include?[10]

The selection of categories of "disability" to be included in the ADA is a matter of politics rather than concern for the common good of all people with disabling conditions. For almost every category of disability, an association has been created for the purpose of informing the public, gathering tax dollars, and raising private funds to research the causes of the disability. Such associations make the disability an item of public concern, and people with each so-called disability and their families marshal funds and attention for *their* disability over others. Competition is part of the politics of disability. A concern for the common good of *all* people with *any* kind of disability is lacking because society is not engaged in what Alasdair MacIntyre would argue are practices whose ends are established by a common good among a people. Instead, public interest is fought for by separate disabilities groups who have little regard for any other kind of disability.

In addition, the ADA fails to provide any kind of affirmative action to back up the legislation. It provides civil rights protection but doesn't guarantee equality of results. In other words, although it may guarantee the right to freedom of expression or the right to enter a government building unaided, it mandates no quotas or ratios in terms of creating employment opportunities, e.g., hiring a certain percentage of people with disabilities in a business of largely non-disabled employees. It actually does very little to give people with disabilities a genuine opportunity to be fully included as citizens.[11] And the separation of church and state ensures that the ADA won't reach very far into the life of any church or faith community. A church is affected by this law only if it has a federally financed day-school program, or if it fires a person because of a disability. The law cannot force a church to be accessible in any way to people with disabilities. Thus the reach of this legislation is nothing like the reach of the Civil Rights Act of 1964.

The Americans with Disabilities Act is now facing budget cuts, as are other programs for people with disabilities funded with federal, state, or local monies. For example, House Republican Majority Leader Dick Armey has been trying to rewrite the law to more narrowly define who is disabled, in response to the flood of lawsuits and complaints that have resulted from the ADA's national building code.[12] In the recent wave of Medicaid cuts, people with disabilities will be directly affected. It is possible that there will be nothing requiring states to cover people with disabilities for Supplemental Security Income.[13] To further complicate things, not only is the movement to give states more control over such programs in jeopardy, but the once popular approach of "deinstitutionalization" is also in danger. For example, consider the community-based programs that were to employ such treatments as psychotropic drugs to help people with mental illness or mental retardation. Senator Daniel Patrick Moynihan recently observed that the increase in mentally ill and mentally retarded homeless people on our city streets is clear evidence that the community-based programs designed to help these people never received the funding or staffing necessary to make them effective.[14]

People with disabilities, their families, and their friends truly believed the story they were being told and invited to live out by the nation-state. They were told they could be independent individuals, free to make choices, to live wherever they wanted, to be masters of their destiny. They were told that science was their friend, protecting them and those like them, and that it was constantly looking for new ways to aid them. They were told they now had civil rights protected by law. By believing what they were told by the nation-state, however, they were actually being made more and more dependent on the state's largesse. Indeed, as they find themselves being made *truly* independent now—free from all the programs and monies of the state—people with disabilities and their families are realizing too late exactly *how* dependent they have been. And they are discovering that, despite their hopes that they would still receive some help, the nation-state really wishes they weren't here.[15]

The Politics of the Church: Rediscovering People with Disabilities as People with Abilities

When we hear the word *politic,* translated as "polity" in many churches, we often assume that what is being discussed has something to do with the politics of the nation-state called the United States. We use the same categorizations, and thus characterizations, of the politics of the church as we do of the nation-state. We believe there is a conservative or Republican way of reading Scripture, as well as a liberal or Democratic way of interpreting the Bible. In this regard, I wish to broaden the definition of politics to include a certain code of conduct that negotiates how and why we live with one another. To this end, the church as body of Christ is truly governed by the politic that it is the "body politic" of God's people. Because it is the body of Christ, it is constituted by a certain kind of discipline that creates the capacity of God's people to resist the disciplines of the body associated with the nation-state.[16]

Granted, it is hard to see *how* the church's politics are any different from those of the nation-state. Farmer and writer Wendell Berry notes that this is because that church has truly become at home in the nation-state:

> It has become the willy nilly religion of the state and the economic status quo. Because it has been so exclusively dedicated to incanting anemic souls into Heaven, it has been made the tool of much earthly villainy. It has, for the most part, stood silently by while a predatory economy has ravaged the world, destroyed its beauty and health, and divided and plundered human communities.[17]

Interestingly enough, in many conferences sponsored by professional health care associations focusing on services and programs for people with disabilities and their families, the people in need of care have been re-envisioned as "consumers" and "commodities." Gone is the *person* with a disability; enter the *consumer* with a disability—as well as their family, primed to buy the latest technology promising to make their loved one's life easier. Gone is the intricate, mysterious, undomesticated, and unpredictable life of the person with a disability; enter the commodity, the point on a sales chart, the controlled variable, and the target of advertisements. This is an economy of token systems gone wild in the lives of those with disabilities.

This consumerist model has entered and embraced the politics of the church. In many churches, the presence of a child or adult with a disability often depends on whether the church has the money to hire someone to care for the person, to follow the person from Sunday school to worship to fellowship hour, and out the door if necessary.

I constantly hear stories of people with disabilities being excluded from church communities. One involved an adult woman who was "borderline mentally retarded," who attended a Sunday school class at a Protestant church for ten years without ever once being asked to talk. There are stories of infants with disabilities being denied infant baptism because of their disabilities, and children with Down's syndrome and cerebral palsy being turned away from the table where the eucharist was being celebrated, because the priest was fearful of the mess or chaotic scene they might make.

This exclusion of people with disabilities, people who should remind us of the good we have in common—which is of course God—is a sign of just how much the church has opened itself to the practices of a society that does not know God. It is a society that is discomforted around differences, celebrating instead a tyranny of normality, of people who "look just like us." Ours is a society that finds the story of Jesus Christ a wonderful myth but a dangerous truth, for it is a story that puts power in the hands of the helpless. Ours is a society tolerant of the church as a voluntary association for free volunteer-run therapy support systems, but intolerant of the church as an embodied story of the gospel that makes demands on our lives. For the gospel is still unfolding as we are schooled by the Holy Spirit by the lives of those we least expect to learn from. The church must understand that it is the redemptive body of Christ, not by its doing, but as a gift of God's Spirit—a Spirit in control of our destiny. Learning to be controlled by someone beyond our control is best taught by those ordinarily considered disabled. In the church, they become people with abilities as they, and they only, can teach us anew how to depend on one another for life itself. We, the church, can only understand the radicalness of this message in the counter-narrative told and lived out in the Spirit-inspired practices of the disciplined, faithful gestures of God's people.

Where is this church that celebrates the sanctity of *all* human life, life that is indeed created in the image of God? Clearly, it is located in the politics of dependence that are powerfully revealed in the sacraments of both baptism and the eucharist. For in the sacraments of the church we are named by God in God's community, made known to ourselves and one another as we are literally re-membered—by the water of baptism, the breaking of the bread, and the pouring of wine—into the inexhaustible body of Christ. We are schooled into a life of dependence on the tender mercies of God as we begin to see life through the lens of God's peaceable reign.

In baptism, the church practices its peculiar politics, renouncing the false individualism of the world, as well as the powers of evil, and making known to all present and all who came before that the true name of the one being baptized is Child of God. It is truly a sign of God's grace as one dies to self and rises into the body of Christ. When people with disabilities are baptized, they, like anyone else, are told by Word and deed, in the practice of loving gestures exemplified in the community of Christians, that they will be cared for and nurtured by God's people. We are now accountable to and responsible for one another in a new way, for this is the way of Christ. It is the way that God wants it—wants us—to be.

Such politics of dependence, practiced uniquely by the church in the sacrament of baptism, is profound, especially when watching and hearing parents live into their understanding of it. When asked by parents what is the *first* thing they should do in the church with their child with a disability, my answer is: "Be baptized!" Why?

Because then this child will no longer be comprehended as a member of an individual family, but rather as part of the household of God. The child will be celebrated as part of a good we hold in common, which is God. Then the family may remind the congregation that "our" child needs a new wheelchair, or "our" child needs respite care for the weekend, or "our" child needs physical therapy. While the congregation may not have the means to meet such needs, it is capable, through prayerful action, of finding ways to be of great help and practical assistance. For this is the way of Jesus.

Furthermore, in the politics of the eucharist, we are reminded as well as re-membered—through the touch of bread and the pouring of the wine—in the decent orderliness of worship, as the priest or pastor lifts up the elements for all to witness—that the one we worship in common is God. The politic practiced at Christ's Table is articulated in the invitation to the meal, when those who gather are reminded that this is not our table, but Christ's. Christ invites us, sets the divine initiative in motion, engages us in the drama of breaking common bread and pouring ordinary wine "for us and our salvation." At this table, *all* God's children, disabled and able-bodied alike, once baptized, are reminded of what our *real* handicapping condition is—namely our unfaithfulness. Our *true* impediment, our narcissism, is unmasked. At this Table, our very limited vision of the possibilities of God, a vision narrowed by sin, is made known. And the undeniable wounds and brokenness of our mortal souls, seen anew in the presence of the one true Christ, are make painfully real. It is here that we cry in recognition that we are *not* the Messiah. By learning and practicing the gesture of prayer, we let loose and find ourselves laughing at what we don't dare try to understand. God's grace is too wonderful to comprehend, yet too good to be denied, and it sets our feet dancing before the cross of Christ.

As we gather around the baptismal font and join hands around Christ's Table (engaging in what Reformed theologian John Calvin called the "Table Gesture"), we celebrate. We celebrate as we remember the common, gestured practices of the politics of dependence, making visible that which was once thought invisible, namely the church, the living Word of God among us. In the sacraments, as we are embodied by God's Spirit, we remember that a new covenant in Christ's name, by Christ's blood, has reached beyond the abyss that once separated us. All of this happens by God's divine initiative, calling us to participate in a cosmic commonwealth, the realm of God.

This divine realm is made visible not as our destination, but as a lens through which we may understand the world. Not only does it prefigure the church, but often it best illustrates for us what we are after in the chaos of church life. Our "kith and kin," the members of the body of Christ who are considered "disabled," often best teach us the ways of the body of Christ, the ways that lead to the reign of God.

I close this book with a list of the "goods" that people with all varieties of disabilities have taught and are teaching me, teaching us, every day in the common life of Christ's church. In the church, they are no longer people with disabilities, but rather people with abilities that I do not have. I first encountered this idea at a group of Presbyterian Christians with disabilities in Pennsylvania. Some people were in wheelchairs, and others had hearing aids that startled me with unexpected high-pitch screams. Still others had Braille keys, board, and paper in their hands, clicking as I spoke, asking me to go back to the beginning after I had finished my talk; and a couple, both with mental retardation, were holding hands, truly in love. To all these people, and others like them, I say:

You teach us the virtues of constancy and perseverance.
You teach us patience. ˙
You teach us hospitality, hosting our laughter and tears.
You challenge our assumptions about what life is, and what living with others in Christian community is.
You are crossers of borders, showing us new borders we never knew the church had.
You engage us in fitful acts of imagination, teaching us that imagination and creativity are skills and disciplined crafts learned in church.
You teach us of the unpredictability and undomesticated nature of God's love that rules this world. There is hope.

Finally, you teach us that we depend on you, as you depend on us, bearing on your shoulders, and embodying in ways too magnificent for our senses to behold, the church, the body of Christ, as perhaps God means it to be. Thanks be to God for these politics of the body of Christ, which institutes our good.

notes

Preface

1. Jennifer Danner, "Looking Ahead Wins Race, Disabled Athlete Believes," *Sunday Patriot-News* (Harrisburg, Pa.), 23 July 1995, J-12.

Introduction

1. Brian Friel, *Dancing at Lughnasa* (London: Faber & Faber, 1990), 71.

2. What is most confusing about this distinction is that this syndrome is named after Dr. John Langdon Down (1826–96), rather than being descriptive of some notion of hierarchy of intelligence.

3. W. B. Yeats, "Among School Children," in *Modern American and Modern British Poetry*, ed. Louis Untermeyer (New York: Harcourt, Brace & World, 1955), 478.

I. Liturgy

1. Or Episcopal.

2. "AAMR Board Approves New M.R. Definition," *AAMR News & Notes* 5 (July/August 1992): 1.

3. Victor Turner, *The Ritual Process* (Ithaca, N.Y.: Cornell University Press, 1982), 131–65.

4. See Edward Robinson, *The Original Vision* (New York: Seabury Press, 1983).

5. Jerome Berryman, *Godly Play* (San Francisco: HarperCollins, 1991).

6. Jean Vanier, *Community and Growth* (Mahwah, N.J.: Paulist Press, 1979).

2. The Radical Edge of Baptism

1. J. A. Davidson, quoted in Donald Macleod, *Presbyterian Worship* (Atlanta: John Knox Press, 1980), 43.

2. Ibid., 44.

3. *Book of Order* (Louisville: Office of the General Assembly of the Presbyterian Church, USA, 1994), W-2.300.

4. John Calvin, *Institutes of the Christian Religion*, ed. John T. McNeill (Philadelphia: Westminster Press, 1960), Book IV, XIV, 6, p. 1281.

5. In the Westminster Confession of Faith, it is written; "The efficacy of Baptism is not tied to that moment of time wherein it is administered; yet notwithstanding, by the right use of this ordinance the grace promised is not only offered, but really exhibited and conferred by the Holy Ghost, to such as that grace belongeth unto, according to the counsel of God's own will, in his appointed time." *Book of Confessions* (Louisville: Office of the General Assembly of the Presbyterian Church, USA, 1993), 6.159.

6. John Calvin, *Institutes of the Christian Religion* (Philadelphia: Westminster Press, 1960), Book IV: XVI:21 (XXI), p. 1344.

7. *Book of Common Worship* (Louisville: Westminster John Knox Press, 1993), 414.

8. *Book of Order*, W-2.3006.

9. Both authors recognize that the labels applied to and practiced upon those considered "developmentally delayed" keep on shifting in American society, from "mental retardation" to "mental handicaps."

10. *Book of Order*, W-2.3009.

11. John Baillie, *The Theology of the Sacraments and Other Papers* (New York: Scribner's, 1957), 83.

12. Ibid., 82.

13. *Book of Common Worship*, 406.

14. Ibid., 408.

3. Teaching Anew the Table Gesture

1. Evelyn Underhill, *Worship* (New York: Harper & Brothers, 1957), 291. I thank Dr. Ann Hoch for directing me to this reading of gestures.

2. Ibid.

3. *Book of Common Worship* (Louisville: Westminster John Knox, 1993), 43.

4. Ibid.

5. William Willimon, "Christian Ethics," *Theology Today* 52, no. 3 (October 1995): 369.

6. Stanley Hauerwas, "Gesture of a Truthful Story," *Theology Today* 42, no. 2 (July 1985): 187.

7. *Book of Common Worship*, 68.

8. Frederick Buechner, *Wishful Thinking* (New York: Harper & Row, 1973), 6.

9. Westminster Shorter Catechism.

10. John Calvin, *Institutes*, 4.14.22.

11. Nicholas Wolterstorff, "Not Presence but Action: Calvin on Sacraments," *Perspectives* 9, no. 3 (March 1994): 21.

12. Ibid., 22.

13. Rodney Clapp, *Families at the Crossroads* (Downers Grove, Ill.: InterVarsity Press, 1993), 134, 147.

4. Practice Your Hearing!

1. Henry Kisor, *What's That Pig Outdoors?: A Memoir of Deafness* (New York: HarperCollins, 1990), xvi.

2. Ibid., 11.

3. I must admit that there is great confusion over hearing or listening to what someone is saying, and building up discriminatory abilities to comprehend what one is listening to or hearing. This is more an intellectual maturation process than the physiological ability to direct our hearing, as there is no auditory muscle, not even the ear drum, that we can bend to our will.

5. Make Way for Electric-Blue Wheelchairs!

1. The name of this child is fictitious.

6. The Abilities Disabilities Make Possible

1. Annie Dillard, *Teaching a Stone to Talk* (New York: Harper & Row, 1982), 40.

2. Miller Williams, "The Ones That Are Thrown Out," in *Despite This Flesh: The Disabled in Stories and Poems*, ed. Vassar Miller (Austin: University of Texas Press, 1985), 61.

3. Stephen Jay Gould, *The Mismeasure of Man* (New York: W. W. Norton, 1981), 151.

4. Stanley Hauerwas and William Willimon, *Resident Aliens* (Nashville: Abingdon Press, 1989).

8. Let the Little Children Come to Me

1. All names are changed for reasons of confidentiality.

2. I have used some of these stories in other publications. It goes to show there are many ways stories teach us long after they've been told.

9. Open House

1. Scott Walker, *The Graywolf Annual Eight: The New Family* (St. Paul: Graywolf, 1991), 4.
2. Stephanie Coontz, *The Ways We Never Were* (New York: Basic Books, 1992), 17.
3. Ibid.
4. Judith Stacey, *Brave New Families* (New York: Basic Books, 1990), 6, 7.
5. Clapp, *Families at the Crossroads*, chap. 1.
6. Janet Fishburn, *Confronting the Idolatry of the Family* (Nashville: Abingdon Press, 1991), 19–36.
7. Clapp, *Families at the Crossroads*.
8. Ibid., 44–46.
9. Names have been changed for reasons of confidentiality.
10. "God has made you a member of the household of God, to share with us in the priesthood of Christ." From the *Book of Common Worship* (Louisville: Westminster John Knox, 1993), 414.

11. The Place and Power of Acceptance

1. Seward Hiltner, *Preface to Pastoral Theology* (Nashville: Abingdon Press, 1985), 27.
2. J. J. Gallagher, "The Sacred and Profane Uses of Labeling," *Mental Retardation* 14 (1976): 3–7.
3. Jo Campling, *Images of Ourselves* (Boston: Routledge & Kegan Paul, 1981), 49.
4. J. Blacher, "Sequential Stages of Parental Adjustment to the Birth of a Child with Handicaps: Fact or Artifact?" *Mental Retardation* 22 (1984): 55–68.
5. Paul Tillich, *Shaking the Foundations* (New York: Charles Scribner's Sons, 1948), 60.
6. Helmut Thielecke, in Jürgen Moltmann, *God in Creation* (New York: Harper & Row, 1983), 350.
7. Joseph Fletcher, "Indicators of Humanhood: A Tentative Profile of Man," *Hastings Center Report* 2 (1972): 1–4.
8. L. Whytehead and P. Chadwick, "Considerations Concerning the Transit from Life to Death," in *Task Force on Human Life* (Winnipeg: General Synod of the Anglican Church of Canada, 1977), 13.
9. Stanley Hauerwas, *Truthfulness and Tragedy* (Notre Dame, Ind.: University of Notre Dame Press, 1977), 162.
10. Walter Brueggemann, *Interpretation: Genesis* (Atlanta: John Knox Press, 1982), 40–41.
11. Robert Coles, *Children in Crisis: Privileged Ones* (Boston: Atlantic Monthly Press, 1977), 554.

12. Günther Bornkamm, *Paul* (New York: Harper & Row, 1969), 194.

13. Douglas John Hall, *God and Human Suffering* (Minneapolis: Augsburg, 1986), 111.

14. Presbyterian Church (USA) *Book of Order* (Louisville: Presbyterian Publishing House, 1994), W-2.300.

15. World Council of Churches, *Baptism, Eucharist, and Ministry* (Geneva: World Council of Churches, 1982), 2.

16. Ibid., 3.

17. John Westerhoff, "The Way of Living into Our Baptism" (unpublished manuscript, 1987), 2.

18. World Council of Churches, *Baptism, Eucharist, and Ministry*, 4.

19. Gordon Kauffman, *Systematic Theology* (New York: Scribner's, 1968), 499.

20. John Patton, *Is Human Forgiveness Possible?* (Nashville: Abingdon Press, 1985), 186.

12. Letters to a Disabled Church

1. All the names of people in this article are fictitious. However, any resemblance to any people is *not* purely coincidental. The article is a conglomeration of many letters and phone calls I receive from parents of children with disabilities and from pastors and priests. That such correspondence goes on is true. That children with disabilities, and their families, are "invited" to leave parishes only because of a child's disabling condition is true. And that adults with disabilities are also asked to leave congregations because of their limitations is also true.

13. To Play Is to Care

1. All names are fictitious for reasons of confidentiality.

2. Carol Gilligan, *In a Different Voice* (Cambridge: Harvard University Press, 1982).

3. Nel Noddings, *Caring* (Berkeley: University of California Press, 1984).

4. Milton Mayeroff, *On Caring* (New York: Harper & Row, 1971).

5. Morton Kelsey, *Caring: How Can We Love One Another?* (Mahwah, N.J.: Paulist Press, 1981).

6. Stanley Hauerwas, quoted in *The Encyclopedia of Bioethics,* vol. 1, ed. W. T. Reich (New York: Free Press, 1978).

7. Vivian Paley, *The Boy Who Would Be a Helicopter* (Cambridge: Harvard University Press, 1990).

8. In l'Arche, care workers are known as assistants.

9. Susan Foster, *The Politics of Caring* (Philadelphia: Falmer Press, 1987).

10. Alasdair MacIntyre, *After Virtue*, 2d ed. (Notre Dame, Ind.: University of Notre Dame Press, 1984).

11. Bruno Bettelheim, *A Good Enough Parent* (New York: Vintage Press, 1987).

12. Vanier, *Community and Growth*.

13. Bettelheim, *A Good Enough Parent*.

14. Robert Bellah, R. Madsen, W. Sullivan, A. Swidler, and S. Tipton, *Habits of the Heart* (Berkeley: University of California Press, 1985).

15. Bettelheim, *A Good Enough Parent*.

16. Jerome Berryman, *Godly Play* (San Francisco: HarperCollins, 1991).

17. Robert Bly, *Iron John* (Reading, Mass.: Addison-Wesley, 1990).

18. Erik Erikson, *Childhood and Society* (New York: W. W. Norton, 1963).

19. A. Fluegelman, *The New Games Book* (San Francisco: Headlands Press, 1976).

14. L'Arche: A Caring Community

1. David Clark, *The Liberation of the Church* (Birmingham, U.K.: National Centre for Christian Communities and Networks, 1984).

2. K. Grunnewald, "The Intellectually Handicapped in Sweden," *Current Sweden*, no. 86 (1986): 86.

3. Vanier, *Community and Growth*.

4. The names have been changed for confidentiality.

5. Jean Vanier, *The Challenge of L'Arche* (Minneapolis: Winston Press, 1981).

6. Vanier, *Community and Growth*.

7. Ibid.

8. Ibid.

9. Ibid.

10. Ibid.

11. R. Collins, "The Non-Rational Foundations of Rationality," in *Sociological Insights* (New York: Oxford University Press, 1982).

12. Mary Douglas, *How Institutions Think* (Syracuse: Syracuse University Press, 1986).

13. Milton Mayeroff, *On Caring* (New York: Harper & Row, 1971).

14. MacIntyre, *After Virtue*.

15. Barry Schwartz, *The Battle for Human Nature* (New York: W. W. Norton, 1986).

16. Douglas, *How Institutions Think*.

15. The Unexpected Community

1. All names have been changed for reasons of confidentiality.

2. Günther Bornkamm, *Paul* (New York: Harper & Row, 1971).

3. Karl Barth, *The Epistle to the Romans* (New York: Oxford University Press, 1968).

16. The Politics of Dis/Abilities

1. "Mouth: The Voice of Disability Rights," *Utne Reader*, September–October 1995, 107.

2. A version of this chapter was presented as the inaugural Edna K. Miller Memorial Lecture at the University of Notre Dame, South Bend, Ind., 2 November 1995. My thanks to the good people of Logan Center who invited me for this lecture series.

3. Alasdair MacIntyre, "A Partial Response to My Critics," in *After MacIntyre: Essays on the Recent Work of Alasdair MacIntyre*, ed. John Horton and Susan Mendus (Notre Dame, Ind.: University of Notre Dame Press, 1994), 303.

4. Stanley Hauerwas, *In Good Company* (Notre Dame, Ind.: University of Notre Dame Press, 1995), 26.

5. Andrew Kimbrell, *The Human Body Shop* (New York: HarperCollins, 1993), 252.

6. Ibid., 253.

7. Ibid.

8. Ibid., 125.

9. Robert Shapiro, "Who Cares How High Her IQ Really Is?" *U.S. News and World Report*, 11 September 1995, 59.

10. Robert Shapiro, *No Pity* (New York: Random House, 1993), 7.

11. Ibid., 104.

12. Kim Mills, "ADA Still Gets Mixed Reviews," *News and Observer*, 23 August 1995, 6D.

13. Dennis Patterson, "Advocates for the Disabled Fight Medicaid Cuts," *News and Observer* (Raleigh, N.C.), 24 October 1995, 3A.

14. George Will, "Welfare: Take Care," *News and Observer* (Raleigh, N.C.), 24 October 1995, 21A.

15. Conversation with Hans Reinders.

16. Hauerwas, *In Good Company,* 26.

17. Ibid., 232.

bibliography

"AAMR Board Approves New M.R. Definition." *AAMR News and Notes* (5 July/August, 1992): 1.

Baillie, John. *The Theology of the Sacraments and Other Papers.* New York: Charles Scribners' Sons, 1957.

Barth, Karl. *The Epistle to the Romans.* New York: Oxford University Press, 1968.

Bellah, Robert, R. Madsen, W. Sullivan, A. Swidler, and S. Tipton. *Habits of the Heart.* Berkeley: University of California Press, 1985.

Berryman, Jerome. *Godly Play.* New York: HarperCollins, 1991.

Bettelheim, Bruno. *A Good Enough Parent.* New York: Vintage Press, 1987.

Blacher, J. "Sequential Stages of Parental Adjustment to the Birth of a Child with Handicaps: Fact or Artifact?" *Mental Retardation* 22 (1984): 55–68.

Bly, Robert. *Iron John.* Reading, Mass.: Addison-Wesley, 1990.

Book of Common Worship. Louisville: Westminster John Knox Press, 1993.

Book of Confessions. Louisville: Office of the General Assembly of the Presbyterian Church, USA, 1993.

Book of Order: 1993–1994. Louisville: Office of the General Assembly of the Presbyterian Church, USA, 1994. W-2.300.

Bornkamm, Günther. *Paul.* New York: Harper & Row, 1971.

Brueggemann, Walter. *Interpretation: Genesis.* Atlanta: John Knox Press, 1982.

Buechner, Frederick. *Wishful Thinking.* New York: Harper & Row, 1973.

Calvin, John. *Institutes of the Christian Religion.* Edited by John T. McNeill. Philadelphia: Westminster Press, 1960.

Campling, Jo. *Images of Ourselves.* Boston: Routledge & Kegan Paul, 1981.

Clapp, Rodney. *Families at the Crossroads.* Downers Grove, Ill.: InterVarsity Press, 1993.

Clark, David. *The Liberation of the Church*. Birmingham, U.K.: National Centre for Christian Communities and Networks, 1984.

Coles, Robert. *Children in Crisis: Privileged Ones*. Boston: Atlantic Monthly Press, 1977.

Collins, R. "The Non-Rational Foundations of Rationality." In *Sociological Insights*. New York: Oxford University Press, 1982.

Coontz, Stephanie. *The Ways We Never Were*. New York: Basic Books, 1992.

Danner, Jennifer. "Looking Ahead Wins Race, Disabled Athlete Believes." *Sunday Patriot-News* (Harrisburg, Pa.), 23 July 1995, J-12.

Dillard, Annie. *Teaching a Stone to Talk*. New York: Harper & Row, 1982.

Douglas, Mary. *How Institutions Think*. Syracuse, N.Y.: Syracuse University Press, 1986.

Erikson, Erik. *Childhood and Society*. New York: W. W. Norton, 1963.

Fishburn, Janet. *Confronting the Idolatry of Family*. Nashville: Abingdon, 1991.

Fletcher, Joseph. "Indicators of Humanhood: A Tentative Profile of Man." *Hastings Center Report* 2 (1972): 1-4.

Fluegelman, A. *The New Games Book*. San Francisco: Headlands Press, 1976.

Foster, Susan. *The Politics of Caring*. Philadelphia: Falmer Press, 1987.

Friel, Brian. *Dancing at Lughnasa*. London: Faber & Faber, 1990.

Gallagher, J. J. "The Sacred and Profane Uses of Labeling." *Mental Retardation* 14 (1976): 3-7.

Gilligan, Carol. *In a Different Voice*. Cambridge: Harvard University Press, 1982.

Gould, Stephen Jay. *The Mismeasure of Man*. New York: W. W. Norton, 1981.

Grunnewald, K. "The Intellectually Handicapped in Sweden." *Current Sweden*, no. 86 (1986).

Hall, Douglas John. *God and Human Suffering*. Minneapolis: Augsburg Publishing House, 1986.

Hauerwas, Stanley. Quoted in *The Encyclopedia of Bioethics*, vol. I, edited by W. T. Reich. New York: Free Press, 1978.

———. "Gesture of a Truthful Story." *Theology Today* 42, no. 2 (July 1985).

———. *In Good Company*. Notre Dame, Ind.: University of Notre Dame Press, 1995.

———. *Truthfulness and Tragedy*. Notre Dame, Ind.: University of Notre Dame Press, 1972.

Hauerwas, Stanley, and William Willimon. *Resident Aliens*. Nashville: Abingdon Press, 1989.

Hiltner, Stewart. *Preface to Pastoral Theology*. Nashville: Abingdon Press, 1985.

Kauffman, Gordon. *Systematic Theology*. New York: Scribner's, 1968.

Kelsey, Morton. *Caring: How Can We Love One Another?* Mahwah, N.J.: Paulist Press, 1981.

Kimbrell, Andrew. *The Human Body Shop*. New York: HarperCollins, 1993.

Kisor, Henry. *What's That Pig Outdoors?* New York: HarperCollins, 1990.

Macleod, Donald. *Presbyterian Worship*. Atlanta: John Knox Press, 1980.

MacIntyre, Alasdair. *After Virtue*. 2d ed. Notre Dame, Ind.: University of Notre Dame Press, 1984.

———. "A Partial Response to my Critics." In *After MacIntyre: Essays on the Recent Work of AlasdairMacIntyre,* edited by John Horton and Susan Mendus. Notre Dame, Ind.: University of Notre Dame Press, 1994.

Mayeroff, Milton. *On Caring*. New York: Harper & Row, 1971.

Mills, Kim. "ADA Still Gets Mixed Reviews." *News and Observer* (Raleigh, N.C.), 23 August 1995.

"Mouth: The Voice of Disability Rights." *Utne Reader*. September–October 1995, 107.

Noddings, Nel. *Caring*. Berkeley: University of California Press, 1984.

Paley, Vivian. *The Boy Who Would Be a Helicopter*. Cambridge: Harvard University Press, 1990.

Patterson, Dennis. "Advocates for the Disabled Fight Medicaid Cuts." *News and Observer* (Raleigh, N.C.), 24 October 1995, 3A.

Patton, John. *Is Human Forgiveness Possible?* Nashville: Abingdon Press, 1985.

Robinson, Edward. *The Original Vision*. New York: Seabury Press, 1983.

Schwartz, Barry. *The Battle for Human Nature*. New York: W. W. Norton, 1986.

Shapiro, Robert. *No Pity*. New York: Random House, 1993.

———. "Who Cares How High Her IQ Really Is?" *U.S. News and World Report*, 11 September 1995.

Stacey, Judith. *Brave New Families*. New York: Basic Books, 1990.

Thielecke, Helmut. In *God in Creation*, edited by Jürgen Moltmann. New York: Harper & Row, 1983.

Tillich, Paul. *Shaking the Foundations*. New York: Charles Scribner's Sons, 1948.

Turner, Victor. *Ritual Process*. Ithaca: Cornell University Press, 1982.

Underhill, Evelyn. *Worship*. New York: Harper & Brothers, 1957.

Vanier, Jean. *The Challenge of L'Arche*. Minneapolis: Winston Press, 1981.

———. *Community and Growth*. Mahwah, N.J.: Paulist Press, 1979.

Walker, Scott, ed. *Graywolf Annual Eight: The New Family*. St. Paul: Graywolf, 1991.

Westerhoff, John. *The Way of Living into Our Baptism*. Unpublished manuscript, 1987.

Whytehead, L., and P. Chadwick. "Considerations Concerning the Transit from Life to Death." In *Task Force on Human Life*. Winnipeg: General Synod of the Anglican Church of Canada, 1977.

Will, George. "Walfare: Take Care." *News and Observer* (Raleigh, N.C.), 24 October 1995, 21A.

Williams, Miller. In *Despite This Flesh*, edited by Vassar Miller. Austin: University of Texas Press, 1985.

Willimon, William. "Christian Ethics." *Theology Today* 52, no. 3 (October 1995): 369.

Wolterstorff, Nicholas. "Not Presence but Action: Calvin on Sacraments." *Perspectives* 9, no. 3 (March 1994).

World Council of Churches. *Baptism, Eucharist, and Ministry*. Geneva: World Council of Churches, 1982.

Yeats, W. B. "Among School Children." In *Modern American and Modern British Poetry*, edited by Louis Untermeyer. New York: Harcourt, Brace & World, 1955.